P9-DWH-760

Instant Pot®
Miracle

6 Ingredients
or Less

Instant Pot® Miracle

6 Ingredients or Less

WITHDRAWN

100 NO-FUSS RECIPES FOR EASY MEALS EVERY DAY

IVY MANNING

Photography by Morgan Ione Yeager

HOUGHTON MIFFLIN HARCOURT
Boston · New York · 2018

For information about permission to reproduce selections
from this book, write to trade.permissions@hmhco.com
or to Permissions, Houghton Mifflin Harcourt Publishing
Company, 3 Park Avenue, 19th Floor, New York,
New York 10016.

hmhco.com

Library of Congress Cataloging-in-Publication Data
Names: Manning, Ivy, author. | Ione, Morgan,
   photographer.
Title: Instant Pot miracle 6 ingredients or less :
   100 no-fuss recipes for easy meals every day /
   Ivy Manning ; photography by Morgan Ione.
Description: Boston : Houghton Mifflin Harcourt, [2018] |
   Includes bibliographical references and index.
Identifiers: LCCN 2018024869 (print) | LCCN 2018025875
   (ebook) | ISBN 9781328557131 (ebook) |
   ISBN 9781328557124 (trade paper) |
   ISBN 9781328633422 (trade paper)
Subjects: LCSH: Pressure cooking. | Electric cooking. |
   Quick and easy cooking. | LCGFT: Cookbooks.
Classification: LCC TX840.P7 (ebook) | LCC TX840.P7
   M36 2018 (print) | DDC 641.5/87—dc23
LC record available at https://lccn.loc.gov/2018024869

Book design by Tai Blanche

Food styling by Molly Shuster

Printed in the United States of America

DOC 10 9 8 7 6 5 4 3 2

4500733394

CONTENTS

RECIPE LIST

INTRODUCTION

I've spent hundreds of hours cooking and testing recipes with my Instant Pots. And I've had about the same number of students, acquaintances, and sceptics ask me, "Will the Instant Pot *really* make cooking meals easier and faster?" I look them right in the eye and say, "YES!"

With this book, I'll show you that delicious meals can be prepared quickly and easily without a long list of ingredients or complicated steps. I've combined my decades of experience writing cookbooks and "30-minute meals" features for national magazines, teaching home-cooking classes, and doing extensive work developing recipes for the Instant Pot to come up with one hundred recipes featuring just six ingredients or less.

I don't count **oil, store-bought broths, vinegar**, or **salt and pepper**, since you've probably got those in your pantry already. Any additional ingredients are shown in red in the ingredients list of each recipe so you can write a shopping list with a quick glance. I use common ingredients that most grocery stores carry and often note which brands I find work best.

What you won't find in this book are recipes that rely on cans of cream-of-whatever soups or precooked convenience foods full of sodium and artificial ingredients, because I believe home-cooked food should be just that: home cooked.

I know that your time is limited and you're probably coming to the kitchen at "hangry o' clock." That's why I include information at the head of every recipe that will tell you exactly how much active time (chopping, sautéing) and how much total time you'll need for each recipe.

In more than a dozen cases, I include an option to use either the **PRESSURE COOK** or the **SLOW COOK** function, so you can choose which method works best for your schedule. Speaking of time, look for "Tasty Tip" notes for ideas on making the recipe faster, choosing the best ingredients, or changing up the recipe with additional ideas so you can make the recipe your own and make the most of whatever ingredients you happen to have on hand.

I've also focused on making a lion's share of the recipes in this book full meals all by themselves; they are labeled with an icon at the top of the page. Think Beefy Taco Pasta, Hoppin' John with Greens, Pork Chops with Tuscan Beans, and Shrimp Paella.

Another way to get complete meals on the table quickly is to use the "pot in pot" method. In these recipes, a side dish is cooked in the Instant Pot at the same time as the main, in a separate baking dish or steamer basket—see Chicken and Quinoa Burrito Bowls, Barbecue Chicken Stuffed Sweet Potatoes, Turkey Breast with Stuffing and Gravy, or Fig-Glazed Ham with Dilly Potatoes, to name a few. Check out the Helpful Equipment list (page 18) for info on the few items you'll need to try these multilevel cooking methods. They're definitely worth having to get the most out of your Instant Pot, and they're inexpensive.

The Instant Pot is a great kitchen tool to make side dishes, too. It can make corn on the cob, creamy mashed potatoes, Sriracha and honey-glazed winter squash, polenta, and perfectly steamed artichokes with just a press of the button, so you can focus on the entrée.

At the close of the book, I've included recipes for the best homemade broths you'll ever taste. I've also included handy charts for cooking different types of grains and beans so you can have a pantry stocked with homemade staples with no fuss. A pantry (or freezer) stocked with these items will mean you can have meals ready in minutes.

Armed with this book and your trusty Instant Pot, I hope you'll discover familiar favorites made easy and exciting new dishes to add to your regular dinner rotation, and I hope you become more confident with your Instant Pot. Good luck and bon appétit!

10 TIPS FOR BETTER SIX-INGREDIENT DISHES

1. QUALITY COUNTS

When you're using just six ingredients, the flavor of each ingredient really counts. Use good-quality staples like extra-virgin olive oil, premium packaged broths, meats graded "choice" or better, and fresh spices. Be a little bit of an ingredient snob—it goes a long way to making your meals awesome. On page 19, I've included a list of the ingredient staples you'll come across frequently in this book.

2. GET TO KNOW YOUR APPLIANCE

The programing of your Instant Pot varies slightly from model to model. Read your user's manual to acquaint yourself with the step-by-step programming before you start making recipes in this book. After a few recipes, the steps will become second nature.

Note that I use the **PRESSURE COOK** descriptor (on earlier models the same function is labeled **MANUAL**). The **SAUTÉ** and **SLOW COOK** functions on older Instant Pot models use the heat settings **LESS/NORMAL/MORE**, while newer models use **LOW/MEDIUM/HIGH**. To avoid confusion, I've included both in this book, i.e., "adjust to **MORE/HIGH** heat."

3. GET THE POT HOT WHILE YOU'RE PREPPING

If you're starting a recipe by browning meat or sautéing vegetables, press **SAUTÉ** and adjust the appliance to the instructed heat first, then prep your ingredients while it is heating up. After a few minutes, the Instant Pot will be hot enough to sauté ingredients long before **HOT** appears on the display screen. To test if a dry pot is hot, flick a few drops of water into the pot—they will sizzle when the pot is ready. If you're starting with oil, add a small piece of food—it will sizzle when the oil is hot enough to sauté the remaining ingredients.

4. DON'T DROWN YOUR DISH

Instant Pot recommends using at least 1 to 1½ cups of thin liquid in order to build up enough steam for pressure cooking. With that said, most ingredients release quite a bit of liquid as they cook. This has been factored into the recipes in this book, so you won't see 1 or 1½ cups broth or water in every recipe. In cases where some of the liquid is marinara sauce or canned tomatoes, I specify brands that are thin enough to work with the recipes.

5. DOUBLE-CHECK THE SEALING RING

I have made thousands of meals in my Instant Pots (I have three). But every now and then, I lock on the lid without remembering to put the sealing ring back into the lid. I wait and wait, but the pressure never builds up. It happens even to the most seasoned Instant Pot cooks! I have made a habit of draping the sealing ring over the appliance immediately after washing and drying it so I'll never forget again.

6. MIND THE RELEASE

Some recipes will require you to quick-release the pressure by turning the steam vent to "Venting" to stop the cooking quickly (see Quick Safety Reminders, page 15). This method is used when cooking delicate ingredients (think shrimp, pasta, and vegetables). The cooking time in these recipes has been calibrated for the quick-release; don't be tempted to let the pressure release naturally in these recipes or you may end up with overcooked food. I loosely drape a clean dish towel around the steam vent to dissipate some of the noisy steam.

Other recipes instruct you to let the pressure come down naturally for 10 to 15 minutes and then release any remaining pressure. This is best when cooking big batches of foamy or starchy foods that may clog the valve (like oatmeal or beans), recipes with lots of liquid (broths, some soups), and roasts that will benefit from a gentle pressure release, much like resting meat on a cutting board before carving. Don't skip the natural release time; it is part of the overall cooking time of the recipe, and rushing this step will affect the results.

7. DAIRY DON'TS

Dairy products will curdle and scorch under direct heat in the pressure cooker, so I only add them at the end of the cooking process. The exception is when cooking with the pot-in-pot method, where the ingredients are cooked more gently.

8. GET THE FAT OUT

When cooking fatty meats in the pressure cooker, you'll need to remove the excess fat in the cooking liquid or you'll end up with a greasy dish. When there's a small amount of fat (chicken dishes, for instance), I include instructions on how to ladle off the fat while it's still in the pot. When there's quite a bit of fat (hello, brisket!), I include the option of straining the sauce through a fat separator (see Helpful Equipment, page 18) before finishing the sauce. Taking this extra step will make for better sauces and tastier meals.

9. THICKEN AT THE END

Since there's no evaporation in the closed-pot system of pressure and slow cooking, sauces won't thicken or intensify like they do in open simmering and baking. To thicken sauces, it's best to add thickeners like flour or cornstarch after the pressure cooking is done to prevent scorching on the bottom of the pot.

10. STIR GENTLY

The Instant Pot is so good at making foods tender, they can fall apart if you stir too vigorously once the cooking cycle is up! In recipes where this might be an issue, I'll remind you to stir with care; in other cases, you'll transfer the solids to a serving dish while reducing or thickening the sauce.

NOTES ON THE INSTANT POT FUNCTIONS

I use the SAUTÉ, PRESSURE COOK, SLOW COOK, and YOGURT functions on the Instant Pot in this book. That's it! Why? Most of the preset buttons (Soup/Broth, Meat/Stew, Bean/Chili, Cake, Egg, Porridge) use the same pressure cooking process—the different labels are there for your convenience and correspond to factory-set times.

They are handy if you always cook the same things and want the appliance to remember your "usual," but these buttons don't magically know the correct cooking times for any given food, and they don't know when your food is done. Since this book is all about cooking delicious new recipes, I use the manual pressure function.

The **RICE** (which cooks rice under low pressure), **MULTIGRAIN** (which soaks ingredients and then cooks under low pressure), and **STEAM** (which heats up with continuous high heat until high pressure is reached) functions do cook differently than the other preset buttons, but I seldom use them and don't use them in this book.

A BRIEF NOTE ABOUT THE SLOW COOK FUNCTION

You'll find over a dozen recipes that include both a **SLOW COOK** and a **PRESSURE COOK** option, so you can choose how to approach them on your own time schedule. But keep in mind that the **SLOW COOK** function in your Instant Pot does not work exactly the same as traditional slow cookers. Traditional slow cookers utilize a ceramic inner pot and elements on the bottom and sides of the appliance to heat foods. The Instant Pot heats from

an element in the bottom of the pot only, so it's important to use 1 to 2 cups of thin liquid (broth, water) to effectively transfer the heat throughout the ingredients. For the best results, the liquid in **SLOW COOK** recipes should submerge or nearly submerge the ingredients.

Note that the **SLOW COOK** temperatures on the Instant Pot do *not* correlate directly to those of standard slow cookers. The **LESS/LOW SLOW COOK** on the Instant Pot correlates with the "Keep Warm" setting on most slow cookers, keeping foods at or around 190°F. Instant Pot recommends using this setting to keep foods warm or reheat them only; do not attempt to cook foods using this setting.

The **NORMAL/MEDIUM SLOW COOK** setting on the Instant Pot runs at or around 200°F and correlates to the "Low" setting on most slow cookers. The **MORE/HIGH SLOW COOK** setting on the Instant Pot is calibrated to 210°F, which is similar to "High" on standard slow cookers. I use the **NORMAL/MEDIUM** setting exclusively in this book.

And a quick safety reminder: Never use frozen ingredients when using the **SLOW COOK** function. It can cause the temperature of ingredients to hover around the food safety danger zone (41°F to 140°F), which allows bacteria to multiply rapidly, thereby running the risk of causing food-borne illness.

To cover the pot while you are using the **SLOW COOK** function, use the Instant Pot lid set to "Venting," or use a regular pot lid that fits flush with the rim of the inner pot. I recommend the purpose-made Tempered Glass Instant Pot Lid (see Helpful Equipment, page 18) because you can keep an eye on the food inside without lifting the lid. Every time you remove the lid while slow cooking, you lose about 20 degrees of heat. It takes time for the appliance to come back up to temperature, which sets back the cooking time.

QUICK SAFETY REMINDERS

Be sure to read the manual that came with your Instant Pot and familiarize yourself with the safety guidelines before you start. Here are a few quick reminders and tips for using your appliance safely and effectively.

Set up your Instant Pot under the venting hood on your stove. When you release steam from the venting valve, you're shooting hot, moist air into your kitchen (and at the kitchen wall). I recommend placing your Instant Pot on a baking sheet on the stove and turning the stove's venting hood on high to suck up odors when sautéing and to dissipate steam when releasing pressure from the venting valve. DO NOT use the stove burners while your Instant Pot is on the stove.

Never overfill the Instant Pot. Never fill the inner pot more than two-thirds full with liquid. (When cooking a chicken or roast, it's okay if the solid portion of the ingredients is above the two-thirds line.) When cooking ingredients that expand or foam when cooking (beans, pasta, grains), don't fill the pot more than halfway. The recipes in this book take this into account.

Stand by until the pressure comes up. The Instant Pot is a "set it and forget it" appliance, but it's a good idea to keep an eye on it while the pot comes up to pressure, just to make sure everything is working properly. Once the pressure cooking cycle has started (it will beep and display the time remaining), you can walk away and go about your day.

Keep your distance when releasing the pressure through the venting valve. Use a long-handled spoon to move the venting valve to "Venting." Hot steam will come out of the valve quickly and rather forcefully, so be sure to keep your distance. I always throw a clean dish towel loosely around the steam vent like a collar to dissipate some of the steam.

When two-step cooking, cool the lid and sealing ring before resealing the pot. If you are following a two-step recipe where you stop the pressure cooking to add an ingredient, or if you open the lid to check on the food but discover it needs more cooking time, you may have difficulty relocking the hot lid on the machine. This is because the silicone sealing ring in the lid expands as it warms up. If you're having trouble resealing the lid, rinse the lid and ring under cool running water. Once the lid and ring cool, it will be easier to relock the lid and proceed.

Tilt the lid away from you when opening the pot. There's steam and condensation trapped under the Instant Pot lid, so remember to wear an oven mitt and lift the lid away from you when you unlock it. Don't let condensation on the inside of the lid drip back into the pot.

Monitor the state of the sealing ring. The sealing ring that sits tightly in the lid should be springy with no cracks. Depending on how much you use your Instant Pot, a silicone sealing ring should last from several months up to a few years. I recommend having a few extra rings on hand, including one that is set aside for use with dessert recipes only. They're inexpensive and readily available online.

Clean the machine. Just like everything else in your kitchen, you need to keep your Instant Pot clean. Make sure it's unplugged and has cooled down, then use a damp cloth or cleaning cloth to wipe the outside of the appliance and the black recessed rim of the machine, where drips tend to linger. Do not immerse the base of the appliance in water. Every time you use your Instant Pot, hand wash the lid with warm soapy water. To wash the sealing ring (which you absolutely should do with every use), remove it from the lid and toss it in the dishwasher or wash with warm soapy water by hand. If the ring starts to smell like all the meals you've made in the pot, soak it overnight in a solution of ½ tablespoon bleach in 4 quarts water in a large bowl. This may help, but don't worry if it doesn't—an odiferous sealing ring won't affect the flavor of the foods you cook in the pot. The condensation cup in the back of the pot should be emptied and washed with every use.

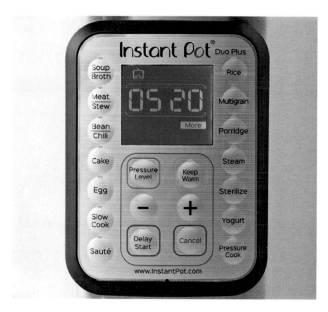

There are handy preset buttons on the control panel. For this book, you'll be using the Sauté, Pressure Cook, Pressure Level, and Slow Cook buttons most frequently.

Use a wooden spoon to switch the valve to the "Venting" position in order to safely release steam.

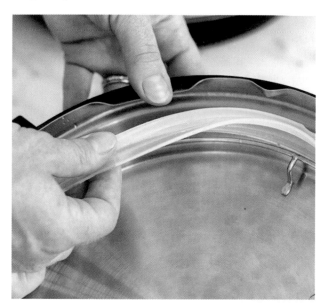

Monitor the sealing ring for cracks. Replace it if rigid or cracked.

Make sure the sealing ring is fitted snugly into the lid before placing the lid on the Instant Pot.

HELPFUL EQUIPMENT

TEMPERED GLASS INSTANT POT LID

This domed glass lid fits snugly on the top of the inner pot and is great for slow cooking because you can keep an eye on foods when using the **SLOW COOK** function. Lids are available from the Instant Pot website and from other outlets online. Be sure to choose the lid that fits the 6-quart Instant Pot.

HANDLED TRIVET

The handled trivet that comes with most Instant Pots is useful for raising food above the bottom of the pot to prevent scorching and to suspend baking dishes above liquid when cooking with the "pot in pot" method. Make sure the trivet is arranged feet-side down in the pot.

TALL TRIVET

In several recipes where the "pot in pot" method is used, you'll need a tall trivet to raise the baking dish above the food cooking below it. (See Chicken and Quinoa Burrito Bowls, page 122.) Look for a stainless steel trivet with 2- to 3-inch tall legs online or at cookware stores.

STAINLESS STEEL BAKING PAN

For cooking one-pot meals with a "pot in pot" setup, you'll need a stainless steel baking dish that fits inside the Instant Pot. Look for a round stainless steel baking dish that is 7 to 7½ inches in diameter with 3- to 3¼-inch-high sides that will fit in the inner pot. Do a quick search on the Internet for "stackable stainless steel pressure cooker insert pans," and you'll find plenty of products that fit the bill. Don't use an earthenware baking dish in its place; it will transfer heat more slowly and won't work with the timing of the recipes in this book.

METAL STEAMER BASKET

A metal steamer basket is useful for cooking eggs in the shell and for steaming vegetables, fish, and meats. I recommend the sort of perforated stainless steel steamer basket that folds up like a flower. Don't use a silicone steaming basket; they tend to conduct heat more slowly and retain food odors.

LARGE SLOTTED SPOON

There are several recipes in this book that require you to transfer cooked foods from the Instant Pot to a serving dish so you can thicken or reduce the cooking liquid separately. In my kitchen, I use a large, perforated plastic scoop comically called a "spoodle," which I got at a dollar store. A metal slotted spoon or perforated ladle will work as well.

LONG-HANDLED LADLE

A ladle with a 9- to 10-inch-long handle is indispensable for serving soup, transferring ingredients to serving dishes, and skimming fat off the surface of cooking liquid while it's still in the pot.

FAT SEPARATOR

Also called a "gravy separator," this inventive device looks like a measuring cup with the spout located at the bottom of the cup. The design allows you to pour off the cooking liquid at the bottom, leaving behind the fat floating on top. I like the OXO Good Grips 4-cup fat separator because it can handle a lot of liquid at once and includes a strainer to catch solids, which makes pouring easier.

LONG, STURDY TONGS

Long (12-inch), heavy-gauge stainless steel tongs are perfect for turning meats as they brown and retrieving items from the inner pot.

INSTANT-READ THERMOMETER

A digital, instant-read thermometer is the best way to check the temperature of meats and for yogurt making. Look for a waterproof digital thermometer online, in the meat department of some grocery stores, and at cookware shops.

FLAVOR-PACKED INGREDIENTS

SPANISH SMOKED PAPRIKA

This bright red powder is made from sweet or spicy red peppers that are smoked over a wood fire. It adds a subtle, smoky flavor. I prefer metal tins (the spice is light sensitive) imported from Spain.

QUALITY FERMENTED SOY SAUCE

Not all soy sauces are created equal. For the best flavor, I recommend high-quality soy sauce that is naturally aged and contains no artificial preservatives or colors. I like Ohsawa Organic Nama Shoyu Unpasteurized Soy Sauce.

ROASTED RED PEPPERS

Jarred fire-roasted red peppers add sweetness, a meaty texture, and pops of color to dishes. Do not substitute diced pimientos, which tend to be mushy and watery. I like Divina roasted red peppers for Italian dishes and love the piquant flavor of Matiz jarred piquillo peppers when cooking Spanish food.

GOOD-QUALITY OLIVE OIL

When I call for olive oil in a recipe, I mean extra-virgin—it's the best quality and the best tasting. Regular olive oil or olive oil blends are made with the cheapest olives available and often have off flavors. You don't need to break the bank; my pick is Costco's Kirkland Signature Organic Extra Virgin Olive Oil, which comes in 2-quart bottles. Store in a cool, dark place—*not* next to the stove.

PACKAGED BEEF AND CHICKEN BROTH

Though I prefer homemade broth, I often use packaged broth for convenience. I like Pacific brand beef and chicken broth (and their bone broth line) and use Imagine No-Chicken vegetable broth. All three are sold in aseptic boxes.

ACETO BALSAMICO TRADIZIONALE DI MODENA

When a recipe calls for balsamic vinegar, I recommend you use real balsamic vinegar from Modena, Italy. Fermented and then barrel aged, it has a rich, figgy flavor that's subtle and not overly as acidic. When in doubt, look at the label; the ingredients list should contain grape must and no caramel coloring.

GRAINY MUSTARD

In a handful of recipes, I call for grainy mustard. I recommend the mellow flavor and lovely texture of Maille Old Style mustard.

DEMI-GLACE

This highly concentrated goop is an awesome way to build up big, long-simmered beef flavor in sauces and soups. Look for More Than Gourmet Classic French Demi-Glace, sold in small (1.5-ounce) packages, in the grocery aisle where the bouillon cubes are sold and online. I always have a package of it in the refrigerator to add a little oomph to sauces and gravies that taste too thin. It's pricey, but a little goes a long way and it keeps for months.

CHILI POWDER

My grandma always said, "Chili is only as good as the chili powder you use." She was so right. I am a big fan of the bright, slightly smoky flavor of Penzeys Chili 3000 powder. Available at Penzeys stores and online.

CANNED TOMATOES

In this book I call for four types of canned tomatoes. I recommend specific brands for specific recipes because they are part of the overall liquid that's needed to build up steam and pressure, and the moisture varies from brand to brand. You don't have to use the brands I recommend, but doing so will ensure that your recipes will cook without scorching.

For zesty recipes, I call for Ro-Tel brand diced tomatoes with green chilies; one 10-ounce can contains 1¼ cups.

For Italian-leaning recipes that call for diced tomatoes with Italian herbs, I like Muir Glen Diced San Marzano Style Tomatoes with Italian Herbs.

In other recipes, I call for San Marzano-style whole tomatoes. These need not be Italian imported DOP tomatoes, I personally like San Marzano-style tomatoes from Muir Glen. They're plump, sweet, and tomatoey and they're fairly budget friendly.

And finally, in a few cases I call for crushed tomatoes with basil; I like Muir Glen brand for this as well.

JARRED MARINARA SAUCE

Consistency varies widely from brand to brand. If the sauce is too thick, it can scorch on the bottom of the pot. I find that Rao's marinara (available online and at well-stocked grocery stores) and Trader Joe's Organic Marinara Sauce are thin enough but also tasty enough to rely on for recipes in this book.

Pacific

organic

free range

chicken
broth

NIC

USDA
ORGANIC

MADE IN SICILY SINCE 1916

MUIR GLEN™

organic

CRUSHED
...DES

MAILLE

ANS
270
YEARS

1747

Old Style
MUSTARD

207g)

Demi-Glace Gold®

CLASSIC FRENCH DEMI-GLACE

MADE WITH VEAL AND BEEF STOCK

Serving
Suggestion

MORE
THAN
GOURMET

Recipe
Included

NET WT. 1.5 OZ. (42,5g) e

Crafted with Pride in the USA

No MSG or preservatives

RO★TEL®

Original

TOMATOES
REEN CHILIES

NON
GMO
VERIFIED

NON
B PA
LINE

Ohsawa
Organic
ama®

BALSAMICO
DENA IGP

SMOKED SPAN
PAPRIKA
LA VERA PAPRIK
Protected Designation of Or

SAFINTER

NET WEIGHT: 2,47oz

FAQS

SHOULD I FUSS WITH THE "KEEP WARM" BUTTON?

I recommend that you turn it off. If **KEEP WARM** is on, it won't affect the time it takes for the pressure to naturally release, but it will continue to cook the food, albeit much more slowly.

I turn it off because I find it too easy to forget about dinner and end up letting the food sit in the pot on **KEEP WARM** much longer than I had intended. No big deal for something like chili, but it can affect the results of more delicate items like chicken.

With that said, **KEEP WARM** is great if you'd like to pressure cook something that isn't easily overcooked (think chili again) and then have the appliance keep it safely warm (between 145°F to 172°F) for 24 hours. It's great for nights when you want dinner the moment you walk in the door after a long day at work.

To turn off "Keep Warm" in newer models (Ultra, Duo Plus), simply press the **KEEP WARM** button when programming the appliance. For older models (Duo), press the cooking program button (usually **PRESSURE COOK** in this book) twice before the cooking program starts.

I'M TIRED OF ALL THE BEEPS! HOW DO I TELL MY INSTANT POT TO ZIP IT?

For Duo and Duo Plus, press and hold the "–" button until the screen displays "S OFF." To turn the sound back on, press and hold the "+" button until the screen reads "S ON."

For the Ultra and Smart models, press and hold the dial knob for 5 seconds until you see the "Sound, Temp Unit, and Alt" screen, then toggle to the Sound setting, turn the dial to "OFF," and press the dial to select.

WHEN I TRIED TO QUICK-RELEASE THE STEAM, IT SPEWED GREASY LIQUID EVERYWHERE. WHY?

When the pot is very full, the steam may contain some fat or starches that will be released along with the steam through the release vent. If this happens, switch the vent back to "Sealing," and let the pressure come down naturally for at least 10 minutes before trying again. You can hasten the natural pressure release by wrapping a cold damp towel on top of the lid. If you must quick-release the pressure, throw a towel loosely over the steam vent to help contain some of the messy steam.

IT'S TAKING *FOREVER* FOR THE INSTANT POT TO COME UP TO PRESSURE. IS SOMETHING WRONG? HOW CAN I MAKE IT GO MORE QUICKLY?

If the vent is set to "Sealing," be patient and remember that it takes a varying amount of time for the Instant Pot to come up to pressure depending on how much food is in the pot, if you're using a "pot in pot" or steamer basket setup in the appliance, and the temperature of the liquids used. The appliance will beep when the pressure has come up, and shortly after this, the screen will display the cook time.

You can make the pot pressurize more quickly by starting with hot liquids or by bringing the foods up to a simmer using the **SAUTÉ** function before locking on the lid.

STEAM IS WISPING OUT OF THE SEALED VENT. WHAT'S GOING ON?

It's natural to see a little steam escape from the vent and float valve (metal pin) for a minute or two as the Instant Pot comes up to pressure. But make sure you switched the steam vent to "Sealing." Even the most experienced Instant Pot user forgets sometimes.

STEAM IS COMING OUT OF THE SIDE OF THE LID, AND THERE'S CONDENSATION ON THE EDGE OF THE LID. IS THIS NORMAL?

Steam escaping from the side of the lid is an indication that the pot is not properly sealed. Press **CANCEL**, quick-release any pressure that has built up, remove the lid, and make sure that the sealing ring is sitting flush in the lid. The silicone sealing ring expands as it heats up, so you may need to rinse it with cool water in order to get it to fit snugly into the lid. Reseal and try again. If escaping steam around the lid is a frequent problem, it may be time for a new sealing ring— they last up to a few years, depending on the frequency of use.

THE COOKING CYCLE ENDED, BUT THE LID STUCK TO THE INNER POT WHEN I UNLOCKED IT! IS MY MEAL LOCKED INSIDE FOREVER?

No. The lid and pot are designed to create a seal to trap the pressure inside. At times, this suction remains for a few seconds after the cooking is done and the pressure has been released. As long as the pressure has come down completely (the silver pin in the lid has dropped), it's safe to pull the lid away from the pot to separate them. Generally, the suction between the lid and pot will dissipate after a few seconds.

I GOT THE DREADED "BURN" NOTICE ON THE SCREEN. WHAT HAPPENED? IS DINNER RUINED?

No, it's going to be okay. The **BURN** screen occurs when the Instant Pot senses that the unit is overheating on the bottom of the pot. The Instant Pot will automatically reduce the heat, which can prevent the pot from coming up to pressure.

To avoid the **BURN** (or **OvHt** in older models), follow the recipes in this book as stated—deglaze the bottom of the pot after browning ingredients as instructed, use the recommended amounts of liquids in the recipes, use the trivet where instructed, and follow the brand recommendations for certain products like canned tomatoes and marinara, which will scorch if you use a product that is too thick.

If you get a **BURN** notice, quick-release the pressure, unlock the lid, and stir the ingredients, scraping the bottom of the pot to release any stuck-on browned bits. The ingredients may have some well-browned spots, but they're usually not truly burned. Add ¼ cup to 1 cup more liquid (broth or water), stir, and start over with the pressure cooking instructions.

BREAKFAST

BLUEBERRY CINNAMON COFFEE CAKE

· · · · · · · · · ·

Serves 6

ACTIVE TIME	FUNCTION	TOTAL TIME	RELEASE
10 minutes	Pressure	1 hour	Quick

This moist breakfast treat comes together quickly thanks to Bisquick baking mix, which has all the leavening mixed into it. Blueberries are a favorite in my family, but you can also use fresh or frozen raspberries or blackberries, if you prefer.

FOR THE STREUSEL TOPPING

- ¼ **cup Bisquick**
- ¼ **cup lightly packed brown sugar**
- ½ **teaspoon ground cinnamon**
- 2 tablespoons canola oil

FOR THE CAKE

- 2 cups Bisquick
- ¼ cup lightly packed brown sugar
- ⅔ **cup milk**
- 1 **egg, beaten**

- 1 **cup frozen blueberries**

1 Spray an 8-inch springform pan that will fit into the Instant Pot with cooking spray. Set a tall trivet in the pot and add 1½ cups hot water. (The trivet should sit high enough in the pot that the bottom of the cake pan does not touch the water; a trivet with 2-inch-high legs is ideal.)

2 **Make the streusel topping:** In a medium bowl, mix the topping ingredients together; set aside.

3 **Make the cake:** In a large bowl, whisk together the Bisquick and brown sugar. In a small bowl or measuring cup, whisk together the milk and egg. Pour the wet ingredients into the dry ingredients and stir until there are no traces of flour. (Do not overmix; it's okay if there are a few small lumps.)

4 Scrape the batter into the prepared pan. Sprinkle the blueberries and then the streusel over the top. Place the cake, uncovered, on the trivet in the pot. Lock on the lid, select the **PRESSURE COOK** function, and adjust to **HIGH** pressure for 40 minutes. Make sure the steam valve is in the "Sealing" position.

(recipe continues)

(continued from page 26)

Tasty Tip: If
you have it handy, add
1½ teaspoons vanilla
extract to the cake
batter for a richer flavor.

5 When the cooking time is up, quick-release the pressure. Test the cake with a butter knife; it should come out mostly clean with a few moist crumbs when inserted into the center of the cake. The top of the cake may look a bit moist; this is fine. Remove the pan from the Instant Pot with tongs. Run a sharp knife around the sides of the pan, then unlock and release the sides of the pan. Let the cake stand for 10 minutes. Serve warm.

PECAN CARAMEL CINNAMON ROLLS

· · · · · · · · · ·
Serves 6

ACTIVE TIME	FUNCTION	TOTAL TIME	RELEASE
15 minutes	Pressure	1 hour, plus 20 minutes cooling	Quick

These gooey cinnamon rolls are a great treat when your family is in the mood for some cinnamon-y goodness but you don't want to turn the oven on. It's tough to wait to dig in, but it's crucial to let the rolls cool for 20 minutes after they're done cooking, as they'll become less dense as they sit.

¾ cup packed brown sugar

2 tablespoons heavy cream

½ cup toasted chopped pecans

1 (16.3-ounce) can biscuit dough (such as Pillsbury Grands! Southern Homestyle Biscuits)

2 tablespoons butter, melted and cooled slightly

2 teaspoons pumpkin pie spice or ground cinnamon

1 In a small saucepan, combine ¼ cup of the brown sugar and the cream and bring to a boil over medium-high heat, stirring constantly. Pour the mixture into a 7-inch round metal baking pan with 3-inch-high sides. Sprinkle the pecans over the caramel and set aside.

2 On a work surface, lay four of the biscuits side by side with a little overlap, and then lay the remaining four biscuits in a row below the first, overlapping them slightly so there are no spaces between them. Roll out into a 9 × 14-inch rectangle. Brush evenly with the butter. In a small bowl, combine the remaining ½ cup brown sugar with the pumpkin pie spice and sprinkle evenly over the dough. Starting with a long side, roll the dough up into a tight cylinder and place it seam-side down on a cutting board. Use a sharp knife to cut the cylinder crosswise into six slices about 2½ inches thick.

3 Place the slices swirly-side up in the pan on top of the caramel sauce, placing one in the center of the pan and the others around the edges with space between them; they will

(recipe continues)

(continued from page 29)

expand as they cook. Cover tightly with foil. Place a trivet with handles in the pot and pour in 1½ cups water. Place the baking pan on the trivet. Lock on the lid, select the **PRESSURE COOK** function, and adjust to **HIGH** pressure for 40 minutes. Make sure the steam valve is in the "Sealing" position.

4   When the cooking time is up, quick-release the pressure. Blot the top of the foil with paper towels to remove excess moisture. Remove the pan from the Instant Pot, remove the foil, and place a dinner plate on top of the pan. Using oven mitts to hold the pan and plate together, invert the pan so the rolls fall out onto the plate. Let the rolls cool for 20 minutes before serving. Serve warm.

Tasty Tip:

If you prefer creamy frosting instead of the pecan caramel, beat 4 ounces cream cheese with 1 cup powdered sugar and 4 tablespoons softened butter until smooth and spread on the rolls after they have rested for 20 minutes.

(ONE POT) SAUSAGE AND EGG STRATA

· · · · · · · · · ·
Serves 6

ACTIVE TIME	FUNCTION	TOTAL TIME	RELEASE
15 minutes	Sauté, Pressure	55 minutes	Natural + quick

All the stuff you love from your favorite breakfast sandwich—English muffins, eggs, breakfast sausage, and cheese—are folded into a comforting casserole in this one-pot morning treat. You'll need a 7- or 8-inch round metal pan with a 6-cup capacity for this recipe.

5   English muffins (12 ounces), toasted and torn into 1-inch pieces

1   tablespoon olive oil

12 ounces bulk pork or turkey breakfast sausage

6   large eggs

1¼ cups half-and-half

3   tablespoons chopped fresh chives

    Salt and freshly ground black pepper

¾   cup grated cheddar cheese

1 Spray a 7- or 8-inch round metal baking pan with 6- to 8-cup capacity that will fit in the pot with cooking spray (see Helpful Equipment, page 18). Place the English muffin pieces in the pan; set aside.

2 Put the oil in the pot, select **SAUTÉ,** and adjust to **NORMAL/MEDIUM** heat. When the oil is hot, add the sausage and cook, breaking it up into large pieces with a spatula, until cooked through, 6 minutes. Press **CANCEL**. Pour out the sausage onto a paper towel-lined plate. Return the pot to the appliance.

3 In a medium bowl, whisk together the eggs, half-and-half, chives, ½ teaspoon salt, and several grinds of pepper. Slowly pour the egg mixture over the English muffins, lightly pressing down on the bread so it absorbs the custard. Sprinkle the sausage and cheese evenly over the top; press again to submerge most of the bread in the custard. Cover with foil.

4 Pour 1½ cups cold water into the pot and set a trivet with handles in the bottom. Set the baking pan on the trivet. Lock on the lid, select the **PRESSURE COOK** function, and adjust to **HIGH** pressure for 15 minutes. Make sure the steam valve is in the "Sealing" position.

(recipe continues)

(continued from page 32)

5 When the cooking time is up, let the pressure come down naturally for 10 minutes and then quick-release the remaining pressure. Insert a butter knife into the center of the strata; it should come out with no liquid custard coating the knife. If the pudding is not done, lock on the lid and return to **HIGH** pressure for 1 minute more. Quick-release the pressure.

6 Remove the pan from the pot and serve the strata immediately.

BANANA-NUTELLA STUFFED FRENCH TOAST

· · · · · · · · · ·
Serves 4

ACTIVE TIME	FUNCTION	TOTAL TIME	RELEASE
5 minutes	Pressure	45 minutes	Natural + quick

This rich casserole, layered with slices of challah, hazelnut-chocolate spread, and bananas, takes French toast to the next level. Be sure to let the baking pan stand for a few minutes before serving; the custard will set up a bit as it stands.

8 (½-inch-thick) slices challah bread (8 ounces)

½ cup chocolate hazelnut spread (such as Nutella)

2 large medium-ripe bananas, sliced

1½ cups milk

3 large eggs

1 Thoroughly coat a 7 × 3½-inch round metal baking pan with cooking spray. Set a trivet with handles in the pot and add 1½ cups cold water.

2 Spread one side of each slice of bread with chocolate-hazelnut spread. Layer the bread and bananas in the prepared baking dish in two layers, ending with bananas. In a medium bowl, whisk together the milk and eggs until well blended. Pour the milk mixture evenly over the bread layers in the pan and press down gently so the bread absorbs the custard.

3 Cover the baking pan tightly with foil. Set the baking pan on the trivet in the pot. Lock on the lid, select the **PRESSURE COOK** function, and adjust to **HIGH** pressure for 20 minutes. Make sure the steam valve is in the "Sealing" position.

4 When the cooking time is up, let the pressure come down naturally for 10 minutes and then quick-release the remaining pressure. Insert a butter knife into the center of the baking dish; it should come out moist from the banana and hazelnut spread, but there should be no liquid custard coating the knife. The top will look moist at first; let sit at room temperature for a few minutes before serving to allow the mixture to firm up a bit. (If the casserole is not done, lock on the lid and return to **HIGH** pressure for 1 minute more and then quick-release the pressure.)

Tasty Tip:

For Elvis-style French toast, substitute peanut butter for the chocolate-hazelnut spread.

ONE POT SMOKED SALMON AND PUMPERNICKEL EGG CASSEROLE

Serves 4

ACTIVE TIME	FUNCTION	TOTAL TIME	RELEASE
10 minutes	Pressure	45 minutes	Natural + quick

This delicious breakfast dish is inspired by Nordic smorgasbord sandwiches made with pumpernickel bread and topped with salmon, egg, and dill. I like to use dense whole-grain pumpernickel for a hearty texture, but you can also opt for lighter rye sandwich bread. The casserole is great on its own, or you can dress it up a bit with dollops of sour cream, capers, and thinly sliced red onion, if you like.

2 slices dense pumpernickel bread (5 ounces)

4 ounces hot-smoked wild salmon, broken into bite-size chunks

7 large eggs

1 cup half-and-half

3 tablespoons roughly chopped fresh dill, or 1 teaspoon dried

Finely grated zest of ½ lemon

Salt and freshly ground black pepper

OPTIONAL GARNISHES

Sour cream

Capers

Thinly sliced red onion

1 Thoroughly coat a 7- or 8-inch round metal baking pan with 3½-inch-high sides (see Helpful Equipment, page 18) with cooking spray. Pour 1½ cups cold water into the pot and set a trivet with handles in the bottom.

2 Place the bread in the baking pan, tearing pieces to fit evenly over the base of the pan. Sprinkle the salmon over the bread and press down gently; set aside.

3 In a medium bowl, whisk together the eggs, half-and-half, dill, lemon zest, ½ teaspoon salt, and several grinds of pepper until smooth. Pour the egg mixture into the baking pan. Cover tightly with foil.

4 Set the baking pan on the trivet. Lock on the lid, select the **PRESSURE COOK** function, and adjust to **HIGH** pressure for 20 minutes. Make sure the steam valve is in the "Sealing" position.

5 When the cooking time is up, let the pressure come down naturally for 10 minutes and then quick-release the remaining pressure. Blot the foil with paper towels to remove excess moisture. Carefully remove the trivet-pan setup from the pot and remove the foil. Insert a butter knife into the center of the casserole; it should come out with no liquid custard coating the knife. (If the casserole is not done, lock on the lid and return to **HIGH** pressure for 1 minute more and then quick-release the pressure.)

6 Let the casserole stand for a few minutes before cutting into wedges. Serve with the optional garnishes, if desired.

Tasty Tip: Taste the smoked fish. If it is very salty, you may want to reduce the amount of salt added to the egg custard.

HUEVOS RANCHEROS

· · · · · · · · · ·
Serves 4

ACTIVE TIME	FUNCTION	TOTAL TIME	RELEASE
10 minutes	Pressure OR Slow, Sauté	30 minutes	Quick

This 30-minute one-pot recipe includes a two-step cooking process—first the beans are cooked from scratch under high pressure and then the eggs are gently poached, nestled in the beans, using the **SAUTÉ** function. Be sure to use taco seasoning that does not contain cornstarch or other thickeners (such as Simply Organic Southwestern Taco Seasoning).

1 cup dried pinto beans, picked over and soaked overnight or quick-soaked (see page 225)

4 teaspoons taco seasoning, plus more for garnish

1 cup tomato salsa

Salt and freshly ground black pepper

4 large eggs

4 (6-inch) corn tortillas, warmed, or 4 handfuls tortilla chips

OPTIONAL GARNISHES

Sour cream

Chopped fresh cilantro

Grated pepper Jack cheese

1 Drain the beans and add them to the pot. Add 1½ cups water and the taco seasoning and stir to combine. Lock on the lid, select the **PRESSURE COOK** function, and adjust to **HIGH** pressure for 7 minutes. Make sure the steam valve is in the "Sealing" position. (Or you can **SLOW COOK** it—see opposite.)

2 When the cooking time is up, quick-release the pressure. Drain off most of the cooking liquid from the beans (about ⅔ cup) and discard. Return the beans in the pot to the appliance. Stir in the salsa. Season with salt and pepper. Use a wooden spoon to create four indentations in the beans (it's okay if liquid rushes back in; you're just creating a little space for the eggs).

3 Carefully crack the eggs into the indentations. Sprinkle the eggs with a few pinches of taco seasoning. Cover with a regular pot lid or a glass Instant Pot lid (see Helpful Equipment, page 18). Select **SAUTÉ**, adjust to **NORMAL/MEDIUM**, and adjust the time to at least 5 minutes. Cook, keeping a close eye on the pot, until the egg whites are just set, 5 minutes. The yolks will be runny. Press **CANCEL**.

4 Remove the pot from the appliance. If you prefer well-set egg whites, let the pot stand, covered, for a few more minutes. (The yolks will still be runny.) Place the tortillas or tortilla chips on plates. With a large serving spoon, carefully scoop up the eggs and beans and place them on top of the tortillas or chips. Serve immediately, with garnishes, if desired.

Tasty Tip: To heat corn tortillas, wrap them in moist paper towels and microwave them for 30 to 45 seconds; they'll become warm and pliable in the moist heat. Or heat them individually in a dry, hot cast-iron skillet over medium-high heat until warm. Wrap in foil until ready to eat.

Tasty Tip: If beans tend to make you "musical," try adding a few teaspoons of epazote to the pot with the beans. The herb can help break down some of the indigestible sugars in beans. The grassy-tasting herb is available where Latin American ingredients are sold.

Slow Cook It: Start with unsoaked beans and increase the water in Step 1 to 2 cups. In Step 1, lock on the lid and move the steam vent to "Venting." Select **SLOW COOK** and adjust to **NORMAL/ MEDIUM** for 8 to 9 hours. You'll have more cooking liquid to drain off in Step 2. Proceed with the recipe as directed.

⬠ SPANISH TORTILLA WITH RED BELL PEPPER SAUCE

• • • • • • • • •

Serves 4

ACTIVE TIME	FUNCTION	TOTAL TIME	RELEASE
15 minutes	Sauté, Pressure	45 minutes	Natural + quick

This classic egg-and-potato dish is delicious served hot for breakfast, or you can serve it at room temperature for lunch or as part of a Spanish tapas spread. Make sure the potatoes are sliced evenly and very thinly; a mandoline slicer will help. You can also substitute packaged hash browns for the sliced potatoes. You will need 1½ cups; no need to sauté them with the onions.

2 tablespoons olive oil

½ **medium yellow onion, thinly sliced**

1 **large (12-ounce) russet potato, peeled and cut into 1/16-inch slices, or 1½ cups hash browns such as Simply Potatoes brand**

Salt and freshly ground black pepper

8 **large eggs**

½ **teaspoon smoked paprika**

1 **cup drained jarred roasted red peppers**

1 Spray a 7 × 3-inch round metal baking pan with cooking spray and line the bottom with a round of parchment paper; spray the parchment, too.

2 Put the oil in the pot, select **SAUTÉ**, and adjust to **NORMAL/MEDIUM** heat. When the oil is hot, add the onion and cook, stirring frequently, until beginning to soften, 3 minutes. Add the potato, 1 teaspoon salt, and several grinds of pepper and stir to combine. Cover loosely with the lid set to "Venting" and cook, stirring frequently, until the potatoes are barely tender when pierced with a fork, 4 to 5 minutes. Press **CANCEL**.

3 Scrape the onion and potato into the prepared pan. In a small bowl, whisk together the eggs with ¼ teaspoon of the paprika. Pour the egg mixture into the baking pan over the potato mixture.

(recipe continues)

(continued from page 41)

4 Pour 1½ cups water into the pot and set a trivet with handles in the pot. Place the baking pan, uncovered, on the trivet. Lock on the lid, select the **PRESSURE COOK** function, and adjust to **HIGH** pressure for 10 minutes. Make sure the steam valve is in the "Sealing" position.

5 While the tortilla is cooking, blend the roasted peppers with the remaining ¼ teaspoon smoked paprika and a few grinds of pepper until smooth. Set aside.

6 When the cooking time is up, let the pressure come down naturally for 10 minutes and then quick-release the remaining pressure. Carefully remove the pan from the pot. Run a knife around the edges of the pan, place a dinner plate over the pan, and carefully invert the tortilla onto the plate. Discard the parchment paper. Cut the tortilla into wedges and serve with the sauce.

⬚ ONE POT CREAMY EGGS FLORENTINE

· · · · · · · · · ·

Serves 4

ACTIVE TIME	FUNCTION	TOTAL TIME	RELEASE
10 minutes	Sauté, Pressure	40 minutes	Quick

This creamy egg-and-spinach bake can be adapted with whatever add-in strikes your fancy—add ½ cup bell pepper, green onions, or ham, or substitute grated cheddar or Swiss for the feta cheese. The only constant is the ratio of eggs to cottage cheese, which makes this egg dish deliciously creamy and tender. For the best texture, be sure to let the pan sit uncovered for a few minutes before serving. Serve by itself for breakfast or with a tomato salad for a light lunch.

1 tablespoon olive oil

2 **medium garlic cloves, chopped**

5 **ounces baby spinach**

Salt and freshly ground black pepper

1½ **cups cottage cheese**

5 **large eggs**

¼ to ½ **cup crumbled feta cheese**

2 **tablespoons chopped fresh dill**

1 Place a trivet with handles in the pot and add 1½ cups water. Spray a 7 × 3-inch metal baking pan well with cooking spray; set aside.

2 Put the oil in the pot, select **SAUTÉ,** and adjust to **NORMAL/ MEDIUM** heat. When the oil is hot, add the garlic and cook, stirring frequently, until fragrant, 30 seconds. Add the spinach, 2 teaspoons water, a few pinches of salt, and several grinds of pepper. Cook, stirring occasionally, until wilted, 2 minutes. Press **CANCEL.**

3 Transfer the spinach and garlic to a mesh strainer and press with a wooden spoon to extract as much liquid as possible. Place the spinach mixture in a large bowl. Add the cottage cheese and stir to combine. Add the eggs, feta cheese, and dill and whisk to combine. Add ½ teaspoon salt and a few grinds of pepper and stir to combine.

(recipe continues)

(continued from page 43)

4 Pour the egg mixture into the prepared baking pan and cover tightly with foil. Place the baking pan on the trivet. Lock on the lid, select the **PRESSURE COOK** function, and adjust to **HIGH** pressure for 25 minutes. Make sure the steam valve is in the "Sealing" position.

5 When the cooking time is up, quick-release the pressure. Blot the excess water from the top of the foil with paper towels. Remove the baking pan from the pot and carefully uncover. The eggs are done when a knife inserted into the center comes out clean with no liquid egg clinging to the knife. (If the casserole is not done, lock on the lid and return to **HIGH** pressure for 1 minute more and then quick-release the pressure.) Let the dish sit for 5 minutes and then cut into wedges and serve.

Tasty Tip: Eggs tend to stick to the pan, so be sure to spray the pan generously with cooking spray.

MANGO AND COCONUT STEEL-CUT OATS

Serves 4

ACTIVE TIME	FUNCTION	TOTAL TIME	RELEASE
5 minutes	Pressure OR Slow	40 minutes	Natural + quick

These creamy steel-cut oats are tender, porridge-like, and only slightly sweet thanks to coconut milk, coconut sugar, and vanilla. The tropical fruit topping given here is one option, but you can change it up and add any nut and fruit topping you like, such as simmered apples and cinnamon, fresh raspberries and almonds, or blueberries and pecans.

1 (13.5-ounce) can coconut milk

1¼ cups steel-cut oats

Salt

¼ to ⅓ cup loosely packed coconut sugar or brown sugar

1 large mango, pitted, peeled, and diced

½ cup unsweetened coconut flakes, lightly toasted

¼ cup chopped macadamia nuts

1 Combine the coconut milk, 1¼ cups warm water, the oats, and a generous pinch of salt in the Instant Pot. Lock on the lid, select the **PRESSURE COOK** function, and adjust to **HIGH** pressure for 13 minutes. Make sure the steam valve is in the "Sealing" position. (Or you can **SLOW COOK** it—see below.)

2 When the cooking time is up, let the pressure come down naturally for 15 minutes and then quick-release the remaining pressure. Stir the sugar into the oats. The oats will thicken a bit upon standing.

3 Top the oats with the mango, coconut flakes, and nuts. Serve warm.

Slow Cook It: In Step 1, select **SLOW COOK**, adjust to **NORMAL/MEDIUM** heat, and set for 2 hours. Lock on the lid and adjust vent to "Venting," or use a pan lid that fits snugly on the pot (see Helpful Equipment, page 18). Proceed with the recipe as directed.

WHEAT BERRY AND CITRUS BREAKFAST SALAD

. . . .
Serves 4 to 6

ACTIVE TIME	FUNCTION	TOTAL TIME	RELEASE
10 minutes	Pressure	1 hour	Natural + quick

Wheat berries (whole-kernel wheat) are often available in the bulk aisle at natural foods markets and well-stocked supermarkets and normally require a long soaking period to soften. The Instant Pot makes them tender in just 30 minutes—no soaking required. Infused with a cinnamon stick while cooking, tossed with fruit, and finished with a date and orange dressing, this salad is a sweet whole-grain alternative to oatmeal.

1   **cup wheat berries**

½   **cinnamon stick**

    Salt

2   **large oranges**

½   **cup pitted Medjool dates (4 ounces, about 5 large)**

2   tablespoons extra-virgin olive oil

2   tablespoons cider vinegar

1   **cup seedless red grapes (6 ounces), halved**

½   **cup chopped toasted pistachios**

1 Combine the wheat berries, 4 cups water, the cinnamon stick, and ½ teaspoon salt in the Instant Pot. Lock on the lid, select the **PRESSURE COOK** function, and adjust to **HIGH** pressure for 30 minutes. Make sure the steam valve is in the "Sealing" position.

2 While the wheat berries are cooking, squeeze the juice of ½ orange (you will need ¼ cup juice) into a blender. Add the dates, olive oil, and vinegar and let stand for 10 minutes to soften the dates. Blend until smooth. Cut the peels away from the remaining orange and orange half. Slice the oranges and cut them into quarters.

3 When the cooking time is up, let the pressure come down naturally for 5 minutes and then quick-release the remaining pressure. Drain the wheat berries and transfer them to a large bowl; discard the cinnamon stick. Let cool for 10 minutes.

4 Combine the wheat berries with the dressing, orange pieces, grapes, and pistachios. Season the salad with salt. Serve warm or at room temperature.

VANILLA YOGURT PARFAIT WITH BERRY CRUNCH

. . . .

Makes 7 cups yogurt; serves 4

ACTIVE TIME	FUNCTION	TOTAL TIME	RELEASE
5 minutes	Yogurt	8 hours 30 minutes, plus chilling time	N/A

The **YOGURT** setting comes on the Duo Plus and Ultra models and includes two automatic steps for making your own creamy yogurt at home: The Instant Pot evenly scalds the milk to denature the proteins and then holds the milk at the perfect incubation temperature for 6 to 12 hours so the yogurt will ferment and thicken. It's an easy overnight process, and the results are head and shoulders above store-bought. You'll need a spoonful of store-bought plain yogurt to get the yogurt started; be sure to check the label and make sure it has "live active cultures."

In this recipe, real vanilla bean and brown sugar are blended into the homemade yogurt. The freeze-dried raspberries add a crunchy, melt-in-your-mouth pop of fruit flavor. Look for them at well-stocked supermarkets such as Whole Foods or Trader Joe's.

FOR THE YOGURT

8 cups whole milk (½ gallon) or 2% milk

2 tablespoons plain yogurt with live active cultures

FOR THE PARFAITS

¼ cup packed brown sugar

1 vanilla bean

1 cup fresh raspberries

½ cup freeze-dried raspberries, crushed

1 **Make the yogurt:** Pour the milk into the pot, lock on the lid, select the **YOGURT** function, and adjust to **BOIL**. Make sure the steam valve is in the "Sealing" position.

2 When the cooking time is up, the screen will display "YOGT." Select **YOGURT** again, adjust to **BOIL**, and cook for an additional 5 minutes; this will help the finished yogurt become thicker. You'll have to set a kitchen timer; there's no way to set for boil for just 5 minutes.

3 When the second cooking time is up, remove the lid, being careful to keep the condensation in the lid from dripping back into the pot. Remove the inner pot and place it in a large bowl of ice water. Let the milk cool, stirring with a rubber spatula

(recipe continues)

(continued from page 49)

Tasty Tip: If you'd like thick, Greek-style yogurt, line a strainer with damp cheesecloth or a thin dishtowel. Pour the yogurt into the cloth-lined strainer and set over a large bowl. Refrigerate the setup for 1 to 2 hours. This will yield 4 to 5 cups yogurt, depending on how long you drain it.

Tasty Tip: If using the Ultra model, in Step 1 select **YOGURT**, adjust to **HIGH** heat, and press **START**. The screen will display "BOIL" and then "yogrt" when done. Proceed with the recipe as written. In Step 4, select **YOGURT**, adjust the heat to **MEDIUM** and the time to 8 hours, and press **START**.

once or twice, until an instant-read thermometer reads 115°F, about 4 minutes. Avoid touching or scraping the bottom of the pot, as this will make the yogurt gritty. Discard any skin that forms on the top.

4 Remove the pot from the water and dry the bottom and sides with a dry towel. In a small bowl, whisk ½ cup of the milk with the plain yogurt until smooth. Return the mixture to the pot and place the pot back into the Instant Pot, lock on the lid, and turn the steam valve to "Sealing." Select **YOGURT** and adjust the time to 8 hours.

5 When the cooking time is up, pour the yogurt into clean containers and store in the refrigerator for 8 hours before serving so the yogurt can continue to thicken. The yogurt can be stored in the refrigerator for up to 7 days.

6 **Make the parfaits:** In a medium bowl, whisk together 4 cups of the yogurt and the brown sugar (save the rest of the yogurt to eat later). Split the vanilla bean lengthwise with a sharp paring knife. Using the dull side of the knife, scrape the sticky black vanilla seeds into the yogurt; whisk to combine. (You can save the scraped vanilla pod to infuse flavor into granulated sugar or any custard recipe.)

7 Spoon half the yogurt into four 1-cup sundae glasses or other serving dishes. Top with the fresh raspberries and then the remaining yogurt. Sprinkle with the freeze-dried berries and serve.

SOUPS & STEWS

⬟ ONE POT THAI BUTTERNUT BISQUE

· · · · · · · · · · · · · ·

Serves 2 to 4

ACTIVE TIME	FUNCTION	TOTAL TIME	RELEASE
10 minutes	Sauté, Pressure	40 minutes	Quick

This quick, Thai-inspired soup gets its richness from coconut milk and its aromatic heat from Thai curry paste. I use fresh butternut squash in the recipe, but if you're in a rush, you can substitute two 10-ounce bags of frozen squash cubes to cut down on prep time.

1½ **cups canned coconut milk (do not shake the can before opening)**

1 tablespoon canola oil

1 **medium yellow onion, chopped**

1 **tablespoon red curry paste**

1 **medium (1¾-pound) butternut squash, seeded, peeled, and cut into large (1½-inch) chunks**

1 cup store-bought chicken or vegetable broth, or homemade (page 227 or 226)

1 **tablespoon fish sauce or soy sauce, plus more to taste**

Salt and freshly ground black pepper

OPTIONAL GARNISHES

¼ cup fresh cilantro leaves, chopped

¼ cup roasted unsalted peanuts, chopped

1 Set aside 2 tablespoons of the thick coconut milk from the top of the can for garnishing the soup.

2 Put the oil in the pot, select **SAUTÉ**, and adjust to **NORMAL/ MEDIUM** heat. When the oil is hot, add the onion and cook, stirring frequently, until beginning to brown, 6 minutes. Add the curry paste and cook, stirring frequently, until fragrant, 20 seconds. Press **CANCEL**.

3 Add the squash, remaining coconut milk, the broth, and the fish sauce. Lock on the lid, select the **PRESSURE COOK** function, and adjust to **HIGH** pressure for 10 minutes. Make sure the steam valve is in the "Sealing" position and that the "Keep Warm" button is off.

4 When the cooking time is up, quick-release the pressure. Blend the soup with an immersion blender or in batches in a standing blender with the lid slightly ajar and a towel over the top to prevent splatters. Season the soup with more fish sauce, salt, and pepper. Garnish with swirls of the reserved coconut milk and the optional garnishes, if desired.

Tasty Tip:
If you come across lime leaves in the produce department at the grocery store, snap them up and stash them in the freezer. Add 4 to 6 leaves to Thai curries and soups like this one for a sweet, herbal flavor. Discard before serving; they are too tough to eat whole.

ONE POT # FRENCH ONION SOUP

· · · · · · · · · ·
Serves 4

ACTIVE TIME	FUNCTION	TOTAL TIME	RELEASE
20 minutes	Sauté, Pressure	50 minutes	Natural + quick

Caramelizing the onions builds flavor in this classic French soup, but it takes time. To make things quicker, start caramelizing the first half of the sliced onions while slicing the other half. This soup is so simple, it really is best to use homemade beef broth if you can.

1 tablespoon olive oil

2¾ pounds medium yellow onions, halved and sliced through root end

1 tablespoon balsamic vinegar

4 medium garlic cloves, chopped

1 teaspoon chopped fresh thyme, or ½ teaspoon dried

½ cup dry sherry or vermouth

7 cups Homemade Beef Broth (page 228), or store-bought (see Tasty Tip, page 58)

Salt and freshly ground black pepper

5 ounces aged Gruyère cheese, grated (1¼ cups), rind reserved

½ loaf French baguette

1 Put the oil in the pot, select **SAUTÉ,** and adjust to **MORE/HIGH** heat. When the oil is hot, add half of the onions and cook, stirring frequently, until they begin to brown, 8 minutes. Add the remaining onions and vinegar and continue to cook, stirring occasionally, until there is a deep brown glaze on the bottom of the pot, 4 minutes. Add the garlic and thyme and cook until fragrant, 45 seconds. Add the vermouth and simmer for 1 minute, scraping up the browned bits on the bottom of the pot. Press **CANCEL**.

2 Add the broth, ½ teaspoon salt, and several grinds of pepper. Add the Gruyère rind to the pot. Lock on the lid, select the **PRESSURE COOK** function, and adjust to **HIGH** pressure for 8 minutes. Make sure the steam valve is in the "Sealing" position.

3 When the cooking time is up, let the pressure come down naturally for 10 minutes and then quick-release the remaining pressure. Discard the cheese rind and season the soup with salt and pepper. Press **KEEP WARM**.

(recipe continues)

(continued from page 57)

4   Line a baking sheet with foil and adjust the oven rack so that it is 2 to 3 inches from the broiling element. Cut the baguette at an angle into ¾-inch-thick slices. Arrange the bread slices on the baking sheet. Carefully sprinkle 1 cup of the grated cheese on the bread, and broil until the cheese is browned and bubbly, 3 minutes.

5   Ladle the soup into large soup bowls, top with the cheese toasts, and sprinkle the remaining cheese over the top.

Tasty Tip:
If you don't have homemade beef broth, dissolve 2 (1.5-ounce) More Than Gourmet Classic French Demi-Glace packets in 7 cups water. Find it online and in grocery stores in the aisle where bouillon cubes are sold.

Tasty Tip:
Instead of seasoning the soup with salt at the end, try using soy sauce; it will make the broth darker and it lends lots of umami flavor.

SMOKED SALMON, LEEK, AND POTATO SOUP

· · · · · · · · · ·

Serves 6

ACTIVE TIME	FUNCTION	TOTAL TIME	RELEASE
15 minutes	Sauté, Pressure	1 hour	Natural + quick

This creamy soup is simple—just leeks, potatoes, and cream. Though you can serve the soup without the salmon as a vegetarian dish with some warm bread, finishing it with good-quality smoked salmon right before serving makes it heartier, and elegant enough for a dinner party.

1 **pound leeks (3 large)**

2 **tablespoons butter**

4 **cups store-bought chicken or vegetable broth, or homemade (page 227 or 226)**

2¼ **pounds russet potatoes (3 large), peeled and cut into 2-inch chunks**

2 **bay leaves**

Salt and freshly ground black pepper

½ **cup heavy cream**

10 **ounces hot-smoked wild salmon, skin and bones discarded, at room temperature**

1 Trim the toughest green part and root end from the leeks and discard. Halve the leeks lengthwise, rinse thoroughly under cold water to remove grit between the layers, and chop.

2 Place the butter in the pot, select **SAUTÉ**, and adjust to **NORMAL/MEDIUM** heat. When the butter has melted, add the leeks. Cover with a regular pot lid and sauté, stirring occasionally, until the leeks are very tender, 4 minutes. (The lid traps steam, melting the leeks without browning them.) Press **CANCEL**.

3 Add the broth, potatoes, bay leaves, and ½ teaspoon salt and stir to combine. Lock on the lid, select the **PRESSURE COOK** function, and adjust to **HIGH** pressure for 10 minutes. Make sure the steam valve is in the "Sealing" position.

(recipe continues)

(continued from page 59)

4 When the cooking time is up, let the pressure come down naturally for 10 minutes and then quick-release the remaining pressure. Add the cream and discard the bay leaves. Using an immersion blender, blend the soup in the pot until mostly smooth. Alternatively, blend the soup in batches in a standing blender with the lid slightly ajar and a towel draped over the lid to prevent splatters. Season with salt and pepper, keeping in mind that the salmon is salty.

5 Divide the soup among six bowls. Flake the salmon and place small mounds of it on top of each bowl of soup.

Tasty Tip: For a sophisticated touch, stir a little freshly grated nutmeg into the soup immediately before serving.

CHEDDAR BROCCOLI SOUP

....

Serves 4

ACTIVE TIME	FUNCTION	TOTAL TIME	RELEASE
10 minutes	Sauté, Pressure	45 minutes	Natural + quick

In this comfort food staple, large broccoli florets and sliced stems become fall-apart tender when cooked under high pressure. The addition of a russet potato thickens the soup, while a small amount of cream and cheese added at the end of cooking make it satisfyingly rich without it being over-the-top decadent.

1 tablespoon olive oil

1 medium yellow onion, chopped

1 pound broccoli crowns, florets left in 3-inch pieces, stems sliced

2 cups store-bought vegetable or chicken broth, or homemade (page 226 or 227)

1 large (12-ounce) russet potato, peeled and chopped

Salt and freshly ground black pepper

½ cup heavy cream, warmed

¾ cup grated aged cheddar cheese (2 ounces)

½ to ¾ teaspoon freshly grated nutmeg

1 Put the oil in the pot, select **SAUTÉ**, and adjust to **NORMAL/MEDIUM** heat. When the oil is hot, add the onion and cook, stirring frequently, until beginning to brown, 4 minutes. Press **CANCEL**.

2 Add the broccoli, broth, potatoes, ½ teaspoon salt, and a few grinds of pepper and stir to combine. Lock on the lid, select the **PRESSURE COOK** function, and adjust to **HIGH** pressure for 10 minutes. Make sure the steam valve is in the "Sealing" position.

3 When the cooking time is up, let the pressure come down naturally for 10 minutes and then quick-release the remaining pressure. Add the cream and cheese and whisk to combine and break up the vegetables. Season the soup with the nutmeg and additional salt and pepper.

Tasty Tip: To make the soup vibrantly green and get even more veggies, add 2 handfuls of baby spinach to the soup along with the cream and cheese in Step 3. Blend with an immersion blender directly in the pot. Alternatively, blend the spinach with a few cups of the soup in a blender with the lid slightly ajar until smooth and return it to the pot.

CREAMY TOMATO BASIL SOUP

· · · · · · · · · ·

Serves 4

ACTIVE TIME	FUNCTION	TOTAL TIME	RELEASE
10 minutes	Sauté, Pressure	30 minutes	Quick

Tomato soup is only as good as the tomatoes you use. I love the bright flavor of San Marzano–style tomatoes. You don't have to fork over big bucks for canned, imported San Marzano tomatoes from Italy; there are American-grown versions available (see Ingredients, page 19). Sun-dried tomatoes amp up the tomato flavor. Look for the kind packed in oil with Italian herbs; the flavorful oil can be used to sauté the onions.

2   tablespoons olive oil (or the oil from the sun-dried tomato jar)

1   **medium yellow onion, chopped**

1   **(28-ounce) can San Marzano–style whole tomatoes, with their juice, roughly chopped (See Tasty Tip, below)**

2   cups store-bought chicken or vegetable broth, or homemade (page 227 or 226)

¼   **cup chopped drained oil-packed sun-dried tomatoes**

1   tablespoon sherry vinegar

½   **cup grated Parmigiano Reggiano cheese**

½   **cup heavy cream**

   Salt and freshly ground black pepper

1   **cup fresh basil leaves, stacked, rolled into a tight cylinder, and thinly sliced crosswise into ribbons**

1 Put the oil in the pot, select **SAUTÉ,** and adjust to **NORMAL/ MEDIUM** heat. When the oil is hot, add the onion and cook, stirring frequently, until tender, 4 minutes. Press **CANCEL.**

2 Add the tomatoes and juice, broth, sun-dried tomatoes, and vinegar. Lock on the lid, select the **PRESSURE COOK** function, and adjust to **HIGH** pressure for 5 minutes. Make sure the steam valve is in the "Sealing" position.

3 When the cooking time is up, quick-release the pressure. Remove the lid and use an immersion blender to blend the soup until smooth. Alternatively, in a blender with the lid slightly ajar, blend the soup in batches. Drape a towel over the lid to prevent splatters. Return the soup to the pot.

4 Add the cheese and cream and stir to combine. Season with salt and pepper. Serve garnished with the basil.

Tasty Tip: Chop the tomatoes while they are still in the can by dipping clean kitchen scissors into the can and snipping the tomatoes into pieces.

STUFFED BAKED POTATO SOUP

ONE POT

· · · · · · · · · ·
Serves 4

ACTIVE TIME	FUNCTION	TOTAL TIME	RELEASE
10 minutes	Sauté, Pressure	30 minutes	Quick

This soup gets its creaminess and tang from sour cream, which is added after the soup is cooked (dairy products curdle when cooked under pressure). Just like stuffed baked potatoes, the toppings are adaptable—add chives, steamed broccoli florets, Cajun hot sauce, Swiss cheese, or whatever strikes your fancy!

1 tablespoon safflower oil

1 **large yellow onion, chopped**

2½ **pounds russet potatoes (3 large), peeled and cut into 1- to 1½-inch chunks**

2½ cups store-bought chicken or vegetable broth, or homemade (page 227 or 226)

Salt and freshly ground black pepper

½ **cup sour cream**

1½ **cups grated sharp cheddar cheese**

4 **slices thick-cut bacon, cooked and crumbled**

4 **green onions, thinly sliced**

1 Put the oil in the pot, select **SAUTÉ,** and adjust to **NORMAL/MEDIUM** heat. When the oil is hot, add the onion and cook, stirring frequently, until tender, 5 minutes. Press **CANCEL**.

2 Add the potatoes, broth, and ¾ teaspoon salt. Lock on the lid, select the **PRESSURE COOK** function, and adjust to **HIGH** pressure for 5 minutes. Make sure the steam valve is in the "Sealing" position.

3 When the cooking time is up, quick-release the pressure. Remove the lid, add the sour cream and ¾ cup of the cheese, and stir gently with a rubber spatula until the cheese has melted and the largest chunks of potato are broken down into bite-size pieces. Season with salt and pepper.

4 Serve garnished with the bacon, remaining cheese, and the green onions.

Tasty Tip: If you'd like a bit of zing, add a pinch of cayenne pepper to the soup along with the cheese and sour cream.

CHICKEN AND DUMPLINGS

· · · · · · · · · ·

Serves 4

ACTIVE TIME	FUNCTION	TOTAL TIME	RELEASE
15 minutes	Sauté, Pressure	40 minutes	Quick

This soothing dish is made by first pressure-cooking whole chicken breasts and veggies in broth, then simmering the fluffy dumplings in the soup at the end. The recipe is best when made with homemade chicken broth, but high-quality store-bought broth will do.

1 tablespoon olive oil

1 **medium yellow onion, chopped**

2 **medium carrots, chopped**

2 **celery ribs, sliced**

1 **pound boneless, skinless chicken breasts**

   Salt and freshly ground black pepper

3 cups store-bought chicken broth, or homemade (page 227)

1 **cup Bisquick**

⅓ **cup milk**

1 Put the oil in the pot, select **SAUTÉ,** and adjust to **NORMAL/MEDIUM** heat. When the oil is hot, add the onion, carrot, and celery and cook, stirring frequently, until the onion is tender, 4 minutes. Press **CANCEL.**

2 Season the chicken all over with salt and pepper. Add to the pot along with the broth. Lock on the lid, select the **PRESSURE COOK** function, and adjust to **HIGH** pressure for 5 minutes. Make sure the steam valve is in the "Sealing" position.

3 When the cooking time is up, quick-release the remaining pressure. Transfer the chicken to a clean cutting board and chop into bite-size pieces (the chicken may still be pink in the center; it will finish cooking in Step 4). Return the chicken to the pot.

4 In a medium bowl, mix the Bisquick with the milk until the mixture comes together into a sticky batter. Drop the batter by tablespoons into the pot. Cover with a regular pan lid that fits snugly on top or the Tempered Glass Instant Pot Lid (see Helpful Equipment, page 18). Select **SAUTÉ,** adjust to **NORMAL/MEDIUM** heat, and cook until the dumplings are fluffy and cooked through, about 5 minutes. (To test a dumpling, fish it out of the broth and cut it in half; the dumplings are done when they are dry in the center.) Serve immediately.

Tasty Tip: For added lemony zing, season the chicken with lemon pepper seasoning instead of plain salt and pepper.

Tasty Tip: Add ½ cup frozen peas, asparagus tips, or snap peas in Step 3 for added veggies.

Tasty Tip: You can also add 2 teaspoons finely chopped fresh parsley to the Bisquick mixture along with the milk in Step 4, and garnish the finished soup with additional parsley, if desired.

 # CHILI MAC

· · · · · · · · · ·
Serves 4

ACTIVE TIME	FUNCTION	TOTAL TIME	RELEASE
15 minutes	Sauté, Pressure	40 minutes	Natural + quick

This family-friendly dish is a super-easy one-pot meal. Note that the recipe calls for very lean ground beef (only 5% fat), so you don't need to take an extra step and drain off excess fat. Be patient when browning the meat and onions—the browned bits on the bottom of the pot build beefy flavor. Chili is only as good as the chili powder you choose; I like Penzeys slightly smoky Chili 3000 blend or bright and zesty Gebhardt chili powder.

1   tablespoon olive oil

1   pound 95% lean ground beef

1   medium yellow onion, chopped

1   (28-ounce) can crushed fire-roasted tomatoes (such as Muir Glen)

1   (15-ounce) can kidney beans, drained

1   cup elbow macaroni (4 ounces)

1   cup store-bought beef broth, or homemade (page 228)

2   tablespoons plus 1½ teaspoons mild chili powder

    Salt and freshly ground black pepper

OPTIONAL GARNISHES

2   cups grated cheddar

1   cup sour cream or homemade yogurt (page 49)

1   Select **SAUTÉ** and adjust to **NORMAL/MEDIUM** heat. Add the oil to the pot. When the oil is hot, add the beef and onions and cook until they begin to brown, 10 minutes. Stir occasionally, but leave the beef in fairly large (1-inch) chunks for the best texture. Press **CANCEL**.

2   Add the tomatoes, beans, macaroni, broth, chili powder, ½ teaspoon salt, and several grinds of pepper. Lock on the lid, select the **PRESSURE COOK** function, and adjust to **HIGH** pressure for 5 minutes. Make sure the steam valve is in the "Sealing" position.

3   When the cooking time is up, let the pressure come down naturally for 5 minutes and then quick-release the remaining pressure. Season with salt and pepper. Serve immediately, with the optional garnishes, if desired.

CORN, SWEET POTATO, AND WILD RICE CHOWDER

Serves 4

ACTIVE TIME	FUNCTION	TOTAL TIME	RELEASE
10 minutes	Pressure, Sauté	1 hour 5 minutes	Natural + quick

Sweet potato and corn combined with earthy wild rice make a healthy, stick-to-your-ribs vegetarian soup. Buy pure wild rice, not a wild rice blend, for this soup for best results. Add cubed leftover roast turkey for extra protein, if you like.

4   cups store-bought chicken or vegetable broth, or homemade (page 227 or 226)

1   (1-pound) bag frozen corn

1   large (12-ounce) sweet potato, peeled and chopped

1   medium yellow onion, chopped

2   celery ribs, chopped

½   cup wild rice

1   teaspoon poultry seasoning

   Salt and freshly ground black pepper

1 Combine the broth, corn, sweet potato, onion, celery, wild rice, and poultry seasoning in the Instant Pot. Lock on the lid, select the **PRESSURE COOK** function, and adjust to **HIGH** pressure for 40 minutes. Make sure the steam valve is in the "Sealing" position and that the "Keep Warm" button is off.

2 When the cooking time is up, let the pressure come down naturally for 10 minutes and then quick-release the remaining pressure.

3 Select **SAUTÉ**, adjust to **LESS/LOW** heat, and simmer until bubbly and thickened slightly, 5 minutes. Press **CANCEL**. Season with salt and pepper and serve.

Tasty Tip: For richer chowder, add ½ cup heavy cream at the end of cooking and simmer for 5 minutes.

CHICKEN POSOLE VERDE

. . . .
Serves 4

ACTIVE TIME	FUNCTION	TOTAL TIME	RELEASE
5 minutes	Pressure OR Slow	45 minutes	Natural + quick

This simple soup is just the thing for a rainy night when you want something comforting but don't want to spend a lot of time in the kitchen. Don't skimp on the salsa you buy; it adds a lot of flavor to this soup. I like the bright, zesty flavor of Chef Rick Bayless's Frontera Tomatillo Salsa.

3 cups store-bought chicken broth, or homemade (page 227)

1¼ **pounds boneless, skinless chicken breasts, cut in half crosswise**

1 **medium yellow onion, chopped**

1 **cup green tomatillo salsa**

1 **(15-ounce) can white hominy, drained and rinsed**

1¼ **teaspoons chili powder**

Finely grated zest and juice of 1 lime

Salt and freshly ground black pepper

OPTIONAL GARNISHES

Sliced radishes

Sour cream

Diced avocado

1 Combine the broth, chicken, onion, salsa, hominy, and chili powder in the pot. Lock on the lid, select the **PRESSURE COOK** function, and adjust to **HIGH** pressure for 5 minutes. Make sure the steam valve is in the "Sealing" position. (Or you can **SLOW COOK** it—see below.)

2 When the cooking time is up, let the pressure come down naturally for 10 minutes and then quick-release the remaining pressure. Transfer the chicken to a clean cutting board and shred the meat into bite-size pieces. Return the meat to the soup.

3 Add the lime zest and juice to the pot and season with salt and pepper. Serve with optional garnishes, if desired.

Slow Cook It: In Step 1, select **SLOW COOK**, adjust to **NORMAL/MEDIUM** heat, and set for 7 to 8 hours. Lock on the lid set to "Venting," or use a pan lid that fits snugly on the pot (see Helpful Equipment, page 18). Proceed with the recipe as directed.

TEXAS CHILI

∙∙∙∙∙∙∙∙∙∙∙∙∙∙

Serves 4 to 6

ACTIVE TIME	FUNCTION	CLOSED POT TIME	TOTAL TIME	RELEASE
25 minutes	Pressure, Sauté	45 minutes	1 hour 10 minutes	Natural + quick

Broiling the beef instead of browning it in the pot cuts down on prep time and adds big flavor to this beef-only chili. Jarred mole paste adds a sweet-spicy flavor without a lot of fuss. The chili is thickened with masa, or corn flour; look for it in the baking aisle of the grocery store. Powdery, finely milled corn flour is a good substitute.

2½ **pounds boneless beef chuck, fat trimmed, cut into 1- to 1½-inch chunks**

1 tablespoon canola oil

Salt and freshly ground black pepper

¼ **cup prepared mole paste (such as Doña Maria brand)**

½ cup store-bought beef broth, or homemade (page 228)

2 **tablespoons chili powder**

1 **large onion, chopped, ½ cup set aside for garnish**

1 **(15-ounce) can fire-roasted diced tomatoes with green chilies, with juice**

2 **tablespoons masa harina (corn flour)**

OPTIONAL GARNISHES

1 cup sour cream

Sliced pickled jalapeños

1 Preheat the broiler and adjust the oven rack so it is 3 to 4 inches below the broiler element. On a foil-lined baking sheet, toss the beef with the oil. Season generously with salt and pepper and arrange in an even layer. Broil until the meat is well browned on one side, 6 minutes.

2 Transfer the beef and any accumulated juices to the pot. In a small bowl, whisk together the mole paste, broth, and chili powder. Add the broth mixture, onion, and tomatoes with juice to the pot and stir to combine. Lock on the lid, select the **PRESSURE COOK** function, and adjust to **HIGH** pressure for 25 minutes. Make sure the steam valve is in the "Sealing" position. (Or you can **SLOW COOK** it—see opposite.)

3 When the cooking time is up, let the pressure come down naturally for 10 minutes and then quick-release the remaining pressure. Place the masa harina in a small bowl and gradually whisk in 1 cup of the cooking liquid. Add the mixture to the chili and stir very gently.

4 Select **SAUTÉ** and adjust to **NORMAL/MEDIUM** heat. Simmer, stirring frequently, until thickened and bubbly, 1 minute. Press **CANCEL**. Season the chili with salt and pepper and serve with optional garnishes, if desired.

Slow Cook It: In Step 2, increase the broth to 1 cup. Select **SLOW COOK**, adjust to **NORMAL/MEDIUM** heat, and set for 8 to 9 hours. Lock on the lid and adjust to "Venting," or use a pan lid that fits snugly on the pot (see Helpful Equipment, page 18). Proceed with the recipe as directed.

BEEF BURGUNDY

. . . .
Serves 6

ACTIVE TIME	FUNCTION	TOTAL TIME	RELEASE
45 minutes	Sauté, Pressure OR Slow	1 hour 25 minutes	Natural + quick

This stew gets a rich, meaty flavor from sautéed bacon, well-marbled beef chuck roast, and dry red wine. To save time, this recipe browns just a handful of the beef to build a beautiful brown *fond* (the French culinary term for the base of a sauce) on the bottom of the pan; there's no need to brown all the meat.

5   strips bacon, roughly chopped

3   pounds beef chuck, fat trimmed, cut into 2-inch chunks (see Tasty Tip, opposite)

Salt and freshly ground black pepper

1   large yellow onion, chopped

½   cup Pinot Noir

3   large carrots, peeled and cut into ½-inch-thick coins

¾   cup store-bought beef broth, or homemade (page 228)

¼   cup all-purpose flour

OPTIONAL ADD-INS

5   (3-inch) sprigs fresh thyme, or 1 (3-inch) sprig rosemary

2   tablespoons tomato paste

1 Place the bacon in the pot, select **SAUTÉ**, and adjust to **NORMAL/MEDIUM** heat. Cook, stirring frequently, until the bacon is browned and crisp, 3 to 4 minutes. Press **CANCEL**. Transfer the bacon to a paper towel-lined plate. Spoon off all but 1½ tablespoons of the drippings in the pot and discard.

2 Season the beef with ¾ teaspoon salt and several grinds of pepper. Select **SAUTÉ** and adjust to **MORE/HIGH** heat. Add one handful of the meat (6 or 7 pieces) to the pot. Do not overcrowd; there should be space between the pieces of meat so they will brown instead of sweat. Cook without stirring until well browned on one side, 3 minutes. Stir and cook for a few minutes more. Add the onion and cook, stirring frequently, until the onion is becoming tender, 3 minutes. Add the wine and simmer for 2 minutes, scraping up the browned bits on the bottom of the pot. Press **CANCEL**.

3 Add the remaining beef, bacon, carrots, ½ cup of the broth, and the optional add-ins (if using). Lock on the lid, select the **PRESSURE COOK** function, and adjust to **HIGH** pressure for 25 minutes. Make sure the steam valve is in the "Sealing" position. (Or you can **SLOW COOK** it—see opposite.)

4 When the cooking time is up, let the pressure come down naturally for 10 minutes and then quick-release the remaining pressure. Discard the herb sprigs, if you used them. Place the flour in a small bowl and gradually whisk in the remaining ¼ cup broth. Add the flour mixture to the pot, select **SAUTÉ**, adjust to **NORMAL/MEDIUM** heat, and simmer, gently stirring occasionally, until thickened and bubbly, 2 minutes. Season with salt and pepper and serve.

Tasty Tip: For the best results, cut up your own stew meat from a chuck roast. The "beef stew meat" available in grocery stores is often made up of a mix of tougher, leaner cuts. If your budget allows, buy beef graded choice or prime; these grades have more marbling and will yield better results than lower-graded "select" and "standard" beef.

Slow Cook It: In Step 3, select **SLOW COOK**, adjust to **NORMAL/MEDIUM** heat, and set for 9 to 10 hours. Lock on the lid set to "Venting," or use a pan lid that fits snugly on the pot (see Helpful Equipment, page 18). Proceed with the recipe as directed.

IRISH STEW

· · · · · · · · · ·
Serves 4

ACTIVE TIME	FUNCTION	TOTAL TIME	RELEASE
20 minutes	Sauté, Pressure OR Slow	1 hour 15 minutes	Natural + quick

Lamb stew that melts in your mouth without hours of simmering? It's possible with the Instant Pot and this humble-but-delicious recipe. I use leg of lamb because it's easy to cut into cubes, but you can substitute thriftier, bone-in blade chops, as my Irish grandmother did. Brown the chops in two batches and cook them whole; they will fall apart as they cook, and the bones add flavor and collagen to the broth. Discard the bones before serving.

2   tablespoons olive oil

2   **pounds boneless leg of lamb, fat trimmed, cut into 1-inch pieces**

    Salt and freshly ground black pepper

1   **medium yellow onion, thinly sliced through the root end**

½   **cup Guinness or Murphy's Irish stout**

1½ cups store-bought beef broth, or homemade (page 228)

3   **medium carrots, peeled and cut into 1-inch-thick coins**

1   **large (16-ounce) russet potato, peeled and cut into ½-inch slices**

2   **tablespoons cornstarch**

1 Put the oil in the pot, select **SAUTÉ,** and adjust to **MORE/HIGH** heat. Season the lamb all over with salt and pepper. Add 1 cup of the meat (or the chops, in batches) to the pot and cook, stirring occasionally, until browned, 8 minutes. Do not overcrowd the meat or it will simmer in its juices instead of browning.

2 Add the onion to the pot and cook, stirring occasionally, until the onion begins to brown, 5 minutes. Add the stout and cook for 1 minute, scraping up the browned bits on the bottom of the pot. Press **CANCEL.**

3 Add the remaining lamb, the broth, and the carrots and stir to combine. Place the potatoes on the top, but don't stir them into the lamb mixture. Lock on the lid, select **PRESSURE COOK,** and adjust to **HIGH** pressure for 25 minutes. Make sure the steam valve is in the "Sealing" position. (Or you can **SLOW COOK** it—see opposite.) When the cooking time is up, let the pressure come down naturally for 10 minutes and then quick-release the remaining pressure.

4 Select **SAUTÉ,** and adjust to **MORE/HIGH** heat. Mix the cornstarch with 2 tablespoons water and gently stir the mixture into the stew. Simmer until bubbly, 1 minute. Season with salt and pepper. Serve.

Tasty Tip: Though it's not at all traditional and my grandmother would *not* approve, I like to marinate the lamb overnight in the refrigerator with a glug of olive oil, a few cloves of chopped garlic, and a teaspoon of dried thyme to add another dimension to the stew.

Tasty Tip: Instead of seasoning the stew with salt at the end, try Worcestershire sauce or soy sauce to add depth and rich color to the stew.

Slow Cook It: In Step 3, select **SLOW COOK,** adjust to **NORMAL/MEDIUM** heat, and set for 8 to 9 hours. Lock on the lid set to "Venting," or use a pan lid that fits snugly on the pot (see Helpful Equipment, page 18). Proceed with the recipe from Step 4.

Slow Cook It: In Step 3, select **SLOW COOK**, adjust to **NORMAL/MEDIUM** heat, and set for 8 to 9 hours. Lock on the lid set to "Venting," or use a pan lid that fits snugly on the pot (see Helpful Equipment, page 18). Proceed with the recipe as directed.

⬤ BEEF AND BEET BORSCHT

· · · · · · · · · ·

Serves 4

ACTIVE TIME	FUNCTION	TOTAL TIME	RELEASE
15 minutes	Sauté, Pressure	45 minutes	Natural + quick

In this quick borscht, you build flavor by sautéing half the meat so that it browns in the Instant Pot instead of simmering in its own juices. This recipe uses both the beets and some of their chopped stems and leaves; reserve the remaining greens for another recipe.

1   **large bunch red beets with greens**

1¼   **pounds beef chuck roast, trimmed and cut into ½-inch chunks**

1   tablespoon extra-virgin olive oil

    Salt and freshly ground black pepper

2½   cups store-bought beef broth, or homemade (page 228)

1   **yellow onion, chopped**

1   **teaspoon caraway seeds**

1   **teaspoon dried dill**

1   tablespoon balsamic or red wine vinegar

OPTIONAL GARNISH

¾   cup sour cream or plain Greek yogurt

1 Wash the beets and the greens well. Peel the beets and cut them into ½-inch pieces; set aside. Finely chop the stems and greens (keep them separate) until you have 1 cup of each; set aside.

2 Toss half the beef with the oil and season generously with salt and pepper. Select **SAUTÉ** and adjust to **MORE/HIGH** heat. When the pot is hot, add the seasoned beef and cook, stirring occasionally, until well browned, 4 minutes. Press **CANCEL**.

3 Add the remaining (unbrowned) beef, the broth, beets, beet stems, onions, caraway, and dill to the pot. (You'll add the beet greens at the end of cooking.) Lock on the lid, select the **PRESSURE COOK** function, and adjust to **HIGH** pressure for 15 minutes. Make sure the steam valve is in the "Sealing" position. (Or you can **SLOW COOK** it—see opposite.)

4 When the cooking time is up, let the pressure release naturally for 10 minutes and then carefully release the remaining pressure. Add the vinegar and beet greens to the pot. Select **SAUTÉ** and adjust to **MORE/HIGH** heat. Cook until the soup is simmering and the greens are tender, 1 minute. Press **CANCEL**. Season with salt and pepper. Garnish with the sour cream, if desired.

CUBAN BLACK BEAN AND CHORIZO SOUP

• • • • • • • • • • • • • •

Serves 4 to 6

ACTIVE TIME	FUNCTION	TOTAL TIME	RELEASE
15 minutes	Sauté, Pressure OR Slow	1 hour 10 minutes	Natural

I generally recommend that you soak dried beans before cooking them in the Instant Pot, because unsoaked beans tend to yield uneven results. But I break my own rule here because the beans are cooked long enough to render them fall-apart tender, and the burst beans thicken the soup and make it deliciously creamy. Dried Spanish chorizo adds subtle smokiness to the soup; do not substitute soft Mexican chorizo.

2 tablespoons olive oil

1 **large onion, chopped**

1 **medium green bell pepper**

4 **medium garlic cloves, chopped**

2 **teaspoons ground cumin**

5 cups store-bought chicken broth, or homemade (page 227)

1½ **cups dried black beans, picked over and rinsed**

½ **cup sliced dried chorizo (2½ ounces)**

Salt and freshly ground black pepper

1 tablespoon sherry vinegar or red wine vinegar

OPTIONAL GARNISHES

Chopped raw onions

Sour cream

1 Put the oil in the pot, select **SAUTÉ**, and adjust to **MORE/HIGH** heat. When the oil is hot, add the onions and peppers and cook, stirring frequently, until tender, 5 minutes. Add the garlic and cumin and cook until fragrant, 45 seconds. Press **CANCEL**.

2 Add the broth, beans, chorizo, 1 teaspoon salt, and several grinds of pepper. Lock on the lid, select the **PRESSURE COOK** function, and adjust to **HIGH** pressure for 30 minutes. Make sure the steam valve is in the "Sealing" position. (Or you can **SLOW COOK** it—see below.)

3 When the cooking time is up, let the pressure come down naturally (about 15 minutes). Season the soup with salt and pepper and serve with the optional garnishes, if desired.

Slow Cook It: In Step 2, after adding the broth, beans, chorizo, and salt and pepper, select **SAUTÉ**, adjust to **MORE/HIGH** heat, and bring the liquid to a simmer. Press **CANCEL**. Select **SLOW COOK**, adjust to **NORMAL/MEDIUM** heat, and set for 10 to 11 hours. Lock on the lid set to "Venting," or use a pan lid that fits snugly on the pot (see Helpful Equipment, page 18).

SOUTHWESTERN PINTO BEAN, SQUASH, AND CORN SOUP

Serves 4

ACTIVE TIME	FUNCTION	TOTAL TIME	RELEASE
20 minutes	Sauté, Pressure	50 minutes, plus soaking time	Natural + quick

Acidic ingredients prevent dried beans from cooking, so the salsa is added at the end in this recipe. Use a fresh refrigerated salsa, not jarred, for the best flavor. You'll need to soak or quick-soak the beans before cooking, so plan ahead.

1   **cup dried pinto beans**

    Salt

1   tablespoon olive oil

1   **medium yellow onion, chopped**

1   **tablespoon chili powder**

3   cups store-bought vegetable or chicken broth, or homemade (page 226 or 227)

3   **cups (1 pound) peeled butternut squash cubes (1-inch cubes)**

1   **cup frozen corn**

1   **cup fresh tomato salsa (such as Whole Foods Market Poblano Salsa)**

Tasty Tip: Look for peeled and cut butternut squash in the produce department to reduce prep time. Be sure to cut the squash into bite-size pieces.

1 Place the beans in a large bowl, cover with cold water and 1 teaspoon salt, and soak at room temperature for 8 hours. Alternatively, to quick-soak the beans, boil them in several cups of water with 1 teaspoon salt for 2 minutes. Remove them from the heat, cover, and set aside for 1 hour. Drain and rinse the beans.

2 Put the oil in the pot, select **SAUTÉ,** and adjust to **NORMAL/MEDIUM** heat. When the oil is hot, add the onion and chili powder. Cook, stirring frequently, until tender, 4 minutes. Press **CANCEL**.

3 Add the drained beans, broth, squash, corn, and ½ teaspoon salt. Lock on the lid, select the **PRESSURE COOK** function, and adjust to **LOW** pressure for 6 minutes. Make sure the steam valve is in the "Sealing" position.

4 When the cooking time is up, let the pressure come down naturally for 15 minutes and then quick-release the remaining pressure. Select **SAUTÉ** and adjust to **NORMAL/MEDIUM** heat. Break up the largest chunks of squash with a wooden spoon. Add the salsa to the pot and simmer until heated through, 2 minutes. Serve.

MIDDLE EASTERN LENTIL AND SPINACH SOUP

· · · · · · · · · ·
Serves 4

ACTIVE TIME	FUNCTION	TOTAL TIME	RELEASE
10 minutes	Sauté, Pressure	50 minutes	Natural + quick

This comforting soup takes on a Middle Eastern flair with the help of shawarma seasoning, a blend of warming spices like cumin, coriander, allspice, cinnamon, and pepper. Look for it at well-stocked supermarkets such as Whole Foods, Middle Eastern shops, and online (I love Spice House's blend), or make your own (see the Tasty Tip below).

1 tablespoon olive oil

1 large yellow onion, chopped

1 large carrot, chopped

2 teaspoons shawarma spice blend

4 cups store-bought vegetable or chicken broth, or homemade (page 226 or 227)

1 (15-ounce) can fire-roasted diced tomatoes with green chilies, with juice

1 cup dried brown lentils

Salt and freshly ground black pepper

2 cups baby spinach, large stems discarded

1 Put the oil in the pot, select **SAUTÉ**, and adjust to **MORE/HIGH** heat. When the oil is hot, add the onion, carrot, and seasoning blend and cook, stirring frequently, until the onion begins to brown, 4 minutes. Press **CANCEL**.

2 Add the broth, tomatoes, lentils, 1 teaspoon salt, and several grinds of pepper. Lock on the lid, select the **PRESSURE COOK** function, and adjust to **HIGH** pressure for 10 minutes. Make sure the steam valve is in the "Sealing" position.

3 When the cooking time is up, let the pressure come down naturally for 10 minutes and then quick-release the remaining pressure. Add the spinach and stir until wilted, 1 minute. Season with salt and pepper and serve.

Tasty Tip: To make your own shawarma spice blend, combine 1 tablespoon *each* ground cumin and ground coriander and ¼ teaspoon *each* ground allspice, ground cinnamon, ground ginger, and garlic powder. Store in an airtight container for up to 3 months. Try it on grilled chicken kebabs!

INDIAN RED LENTIL SOUP

· · · · · · · · · ·

Serves 4

ACTIVE TIME	FUNCTION	TOTAL TIME	RELEASE
15 minutes	Pressure	30 minutes	Quick

This filling soup is a staple in India, where it is often served with rice or bread for breakfast. It's finished with a spiced oil called *tarka* and garnished with cilantro and serrano chiles, which are optional.

1   cup red lentils, rinsed

1   tablespoon curry powder

Salt

3   tablespoons canola oil (see Tasty Tip, below)

2   teaspoons brown mustard seeds

½   medium yellow onion, finely chopped

3   medium garlic cloves, chopped

1   medium tomato, chopped

Freshly ground black pepper

OPTIONAL GARNISHES

½   cup chopped fresh cilantro

1   serrano chile, finely chopped

1 Combine 4½ cups water, the lentils, curry powder, and 1½ teaspoons salt in the Instant Pot. Lock on the lid, select the **PRESSURE COOK** function, and adjust to **HIGH** pressure for 10 minutes. Make sure the steam valve is in the "Sealing" position.

2 While the soup is cooking, heat the oil in a small saucepan over medium heat. Add the mustard seeds and cook, stirring occasionally, until the mustard seeds begin to pop, 30 seconds. Add the onion and cook until tender, 4 minutes. Add the garlic and cook for 1 minute. Set aside.

3 When the cooking time is up, carefully quick-release the pressure. Stir the onion mixture and tomatoes into the soup and season with salt and pepper. Serve the soup garnished with the cilantro and serrano chile, if desired.

Tasty Tip: For a richer flavor, substitute ghee (Indian clarified butter) for the oil. Ghee is available in the baking aisle of most grocery stores and adds a rich, buttery flavor to foods without burning like regular butter does.

ONE POT PORK AND MISO RAMEN

· · · · · · · · · ·

Serves 4

ACTIVE TIME	FUNCTION	TOTAL TIME	RELEASE
25 minutes	Steam, Sauté, Pressure	1 hour 10 minutes	Quick

Authentic ramen is all about the savory broth, which traditionally takes days to make. But the Instant Pot makes a rich broth in 30 minutes with a combo of chicken broth (homemade is best), pork shoulder, and miso paste. This recipe includes soft-cooked eggs with runny yolks; cook them for 5 to 6 minutes if you prefer set yolks. The soup is delicious as is, or you can add a few of the no-work garnishes if you're aiming for an Instagram-worthy bowl of noodles.

4   large eggs

1½   pounds pork shoulder, cut into 4 large pieces

    Salt and freshly ground black pepper

1   tablespoon canola oil

6   cups store-bought chicken broth, or homemade (page 227)

4   green onions, thinly sliced, white and green parts separated

3   tablespoons red or white miso

2   (3-ounce) packages dried ramen noodles (seasoning packet discarded)

2   heads baby bok choy, split lengthwise

1 Place the eggs on a trivet or steamer basket set in the pot and add 1 cup cold water. Select **PRESSURE COOK** and adjust to **HIGH** pressure for 3 minutes. When the cooking time is up, quick-release the pressure and put the eggs in an ice bath for a few minutes to keep them from overcooking. Discard the ice water, peel the eggs, and cut them in half lengthwise; set aside.

2 Select **SAUTÉ** and adjust to **NORMAL/MEDIUM** heat. Season the pork all over with salt and pepper and drizzle with the oil. When the pot is hot, add the pork and cook until browned all over, 6 minutes. Press **CANCEL**.

3 Add the broth and white parts of the green onions. Lock on the lid, select the **PRESSURE COOK** function, and adjust to **HIGH** pressure for 35 minutes. Make sure the steam valve is in the "Sealing" position.

(recipe continues)

(continued from page 85)

OPTIONAL GARNISHES

> Nori seaweed sheets
>
> Canned bamboo shoots
>
> Shichimi togarashi (spicy Japanese chile and sesame seed seasoning)

4 When the cooking time is up, quick-release the pressure. Transfer the pork to a cutting board. Using a sharp carving knife, slice the pork against the grain into very thin slices.

5 Select **SAUTÉ** and adjust to **NORMAL/MEDIUM** heat. When the broth begins to simmer, use a ladle to skim some of the foam/fat that rises to the surface (see Tasty Tip, below). Whisk in the miso. Add the noodles and bok choy and simmer until just tender, 3 minutes. Press **CANCEL**.

6 Ladle the soup into large bowls. Top with the pork, eggs, green onions, and any optional garnishes.

Tasty Tip: Japanese diners expect a bit of fat floating on the surface of their ramen broth—it's considered an essential part of the dish. Skim as much or as little of the foam/fat from the surface of the broth as you wish, but keep in mind that the fat is where the flavor is.

VEGETARIAN MAINS

ONE POT LEMONY TORTELLINI ALFREDO

. . . .

Serves 4

ACTIVE TIME	FUNCTION	TOTAL TIME	RELEASE
5 minutes	Pressure, Sauté	30 minutes	Natural + quick

If you love fettuccine Alfredo, you're really going to love this pasta. It's creamy, but a little lighter than the ultra-rich restaurant version. Use dried cheese tortellini for this recipe; fresh tortellini will overcook and fall apart under pressure.

1 pound dried cheese tortellini (such as Barilla Three Cheese Tortellini)

3 cups store-bought vegetable or chicken broth, or homemade (page 226 or 227)

2 medium garlic cloves, chopped

2 teaspoons olive oil

Salt and freshly ground black pepper

¾ cup frozen peas, thawed

1½ cups heavy cream

2 teaspoons finely grated lemon zest

½ cup grated Parmesan cheese

1 Combine the tortellini, broth, garlic, olive oil, 1 teaspoon salt, and a few grinds of pepper in the pot. Lock on the lid, select the **PRESSURE COOK** function, and adjust to **HIGH** pressure for 10 minutes. Make sure the steam valve is in the "Sealing" position.

2 When the cooking time is up, let the pressure come down naturally for 10 minutes and then quick-release the remaining pressure. Add the peas, cream, and lemon zest. Select **SAUTÉ** and adjust to **NORMAL/MEDIUM** heat. Cook, stirring occasionally, until the sauce thickens slightly, 2 minutes. Press **CANCEL**. Add the cheese and stir gently to combine. Serve immediately.

Tasty Tip: Instead of peas, try adding thick asparagus tips, defrosted frozen artichoke hearts, or frozen bay shrimp to the pot.

MACARONI AND CHEESE WITH BROCCOLI

· · · · · · · · · ·
Serves 4

ACTIVE TIME	FUNCTION	TOTAL TIME	RELEASE
8 minutes	Pressure	26 minutes	Quick

This cheesy pasta dish will satisfy your mac and cheese cravings, while the inclusion of broccoli makes it a little healthier (it's optional if you're cooking for picky eaters). You can use either traditional elbow macaroni or rotini pasta here; both cook at the same rate.

12 ounces dry elbow macaroni or rotini pasta

4 teaspoons olive oil

1¼ teaspoons dry mustard

Salt and freshly ground black pepper

1 large (8-ounce) broccoli crown, left whole

½ cup chive and onion cream cheese spread (4 ounces)

1½ cups grated sharp cheddar cheese (4 ounces)

1 Combine the pasta, 3 cups water, the oil, mustard, and 1 teaspoon salt in the pot. Place the broccoli on top of the pasta, pushing the stalk into the pasta and liquid but leaving the florets above the mixture. Lock on the lid, select the **PRESSURE COOK** function, and adjust to **LOW** pressure for 5 minutes. Make sure the steam valve is in the "Sealing" position.

2 When the cooking time is up, quick-release the pressure. Transfer the broccoli to a cutting board. Chop the firm stem into bite-size pieces and leave the florets whole; set aside.

3 Add the cream cheese to the pasta and stir with a rubber spatula until melted. Add the cheddar in two additions, stirring after each addition. Remove the pot from the appliance, add the broccoli to the pot, and stir to combine; the broccoli will fall apart into tiny pieces. Season with salt and pepper and serve immediately.

Tasty Tip: The pasta will thicken upon standing; add a little hot water or milk to loosen the sauce, if desired.

MUSHROOM RISOTTO

·········

Serves 4

ACTIVE TIME	FUNCTION	TOTAL TIME	RELEASE
20 minutes	Sauté, Pressure	40 minutes	Quick

Short-grain Arborio rice becomes creamy with just a hint of chew in minutes in the Instant Pot, no laborious stirring required. I love the flavor of mushroom broth, but vegetable or chicken broth will work here, too.

2 tablespoons olive oil

2 **medium leeks, white and light green parts only, halved lengthwise, rinsed, and chopped**

4 **cups mixed wild mushrooms (8 ounces), sliced**

1 **tablespoon chopped fresh thyme**

Salt

1 **cup Arborio rice**

3 cups store-bought mushroom broth (such as Pacific Foods) or vegetable broth, or homemade (page 226)

½ **cup grated Parmesan cheese**

Finely grated zest and juice of ½ lemon

Freshly ground black pepper

1 Put the oil in the pot, select **SAUTÉ**, and adjust to **NORMAL/MEDIUM** heat. When the oil is hot, add the leeks and cook, stirring occasionally, until tender, 3 minutes. Add the mushrooms, thyme, and a generous pinch of salt and cook, stirring occasionally, until the mushrooms give off their liquid and begin to brown, 7 minutes. Press **CANCEL**. Set aside ¼ cup of the mushroom mixture for garnish.

2 Add the rice and stir to coat the grains with the vegetables and oil. Add the broth and stir to combine. Lock on the lid, select the **PRESSURE COOK** function, and adjust to **HIGH** pressure for 8 minutes. Make sure the steam valve is in the "Sealing" position.

3 When the time is up, quick-release the pressure and remove the lid. Add the cheese, lemon zest, and lemon juice and stir to combine. Season with salt and pepper. Serve, garnished with the reserved sautéed mushrooms and leeks.

Tasty Tip: To strip thyme leaves from their stems, hold the woody end of a sprig between your thumb and forefinger. Gently pinch the sprig with the thumb and forefinger of your other hand and pull down the stem to strip the leaves away from the tough stem. Discard the woody stem and chop the leaves and tender bits.

HOPPIN' JOHN WITH GREENS

ONE POT

· · · · · · · · · ·

Serves 4

ACTIVE TIME	FUNCTION	TOTAL TIME	RELEASE
10 minutes	Sauté, Pressure	45 minutes	Natural + quick

This Southern specialty is served on New Year's Day for good fortune in the coming year. The greens represent paper money and the black-eyed peas represent coins. In this easy-peasy recipe, the rice and beans are cooked at the same time using the "pot in pot" method, making it a great vegetarian meal anytime.

1   cup dried black-eyed peas, soaked overnight or quick-soaked (see page 225)

2½ tablespoons olive oil

1   medium yellow onion, chopped

1   red bell pepper, chopped

3   teaspoons salt-free Cajun seasoning

1½ cups long-grain white rice, rinsed and drained

    Salt

1   bunch Swiss chard, center rib and stem discarded, leaves torn into bite-size pieces

    Freshly ground black pepper

OPTIONAL GARNISH

    Hot sauce

1 Drain the beans and set aside. Put 1½ tablespoons of the oil in the pot, select **SAUTÉ**, and adjust to **MORE/HIGH** heat. Add the onion, bell pepper, and Cajun seasoning and cook, stirring frequently, until the onion is tender, 4 minutes. Press **CANCEL**. Add the beans and 1¼ cups water and stir to combine.

2 In a 7 × 3½-inch round metal baking pan, combine the rice with 1½ cups cold water, the remaining tablespoon of oil, and a good pinch of salt. Place the baking pan, uncovered, on a tall trivet set over the bean mixture. Select the **PRESSURE COOK** function and adjust to **HIGH** pressure for 4 minutes. Make sure the steam valve is in the "Sealing" position.

3 When the cooking time is up, let the pressure come down naturally for 10 minutes, and then quick-release any remaining pressure. Remove the rice in the baking pan and trivet, fluff with a fork, cover loosely, and set aside. Add the Swiss chard to the pot and stir gently to combine it with the black-eyed peas. Replace the lid and switch to "Venting." Select **SAUTÉ**, adjust to **NORMAL/MEDIUM** heat, and simmer until the chard is wilted, 5 minutes. Season with salt and pepper. Serve the rice topped with the black-eyed pea mixture and optional hot sauce on the side.

Tasty Tip: Add 4 ounces diced vegetarian andouille sausage (I like Tofurky brand) to the pot along with the onion for an extra dose of protein.

ONE POT

BARBECUE TOFU SANDWICHES

· · · · · · · · · ·
Serves 4

ACTIVE TIME	FUNCTION	TOTAL TIME	RELEASE
10 minutes	Sauté, Pressure	30 minutes	Quick

The Instant Pot has a magic way of infusing ingredients with flavor—that holds true for tofu as well as meat. My vegetarian husband loves this barbecue-blasted tofu loaded on squishy hamburger buns, but it's also yummy served on plain rice or Spanish Rice (page 210).

1   tablespoon olive oil

1   **medium yellow onion, sliced through root end**

1   **red bell pepper, thinly sliced**

⅔   **cup thick barbecue sauce (such as Kingsford Brown Sugar Applewood)**

2   tablespoons balsamic or red wine vinegar

    Freshly ground black pepper

1   **pound extra-firm tofu, patted dry and cut into ½ × 2-inch sticks**

4   **hamburger buns, toasted**

1 Put the oil in the pot, select **SAUTÉ**, and adjust to **NORMAL/MEDIUM** heat. When the oil is hot, add the onion and bell pepper and cook, stirring frequently, until beginning to brown, 4 minutes. Press **CANCEL**. Add the barbecue sauce, ¼ cup water, the vinegar, and several grinds of pepper and stir to combine. Add the tofu and stir gently with a rubber spatula, taking care not to break up the tofu.

2 Lock on the lid, select the **PRESSURE COOK** function, and adjust to **HIGH** pressure for 3 minutes. Make sure the steam valve is in the "Sealing" position. When the cooking time is up, quick-release the pressure.

3 With a slotted spoon, transfer the tofu and vegetables to a large bowl; cover with foil. Select **SAUTÉ**, adjust to **MORE/HIGH** heat, and simmer, uncovered, until the sauce has thickened, 3 minutes. Press **CANCEL**.

4 Mound the tofu and veggies on the bottom half of the buns. Drizzle with some of the sauce and sandwich with the bun tops. Serve immediately.

Tasty Tip:
The tofu, sitting in the savory sauce, will taste even better the next day.

ONE POT

MIDDLE EASTERN LENTILS AND RICE WITH CARAMELIZED ONIONS

· ·

Serves 4 as a meal, 6 as a side dish

ACTIVE TIME	FUNCTION	TOTAL TIME	RELEASE
20 minutes	Sauté, Pressure	45 minutes	Natural + quick

This simple rice-and-lentil dish is much greater than a sum of its parts. Dark green Puy lentils are cooked in the bottom of the pot with caramelized onions while the delicate basmati rice is cooked with a "pot in pot" method—in a baking dish on a trivet above the lentils so it doesn't become mushy. Top the dish with Greek yogurt or a fried egg for a satisfying vegetarian entrée, or serve it as a side dish for grilled meat or fish.

1   **cup dark green lentils du Puy**

4   cups boiling water

2   tablespoons olive oil

1   **large yellow onion, thinly sliced**

3   **medium garlic cloves, finely chopped**

1¼ teaspoons ground cumin (see Tasty Tip, page 100)

3   cups store-bought vegetable broth, or homemade (page 226), or water

    Salt and freshly ground black pepper

1   **cup basmati rice, rinsed and drained**

1   **cup plain Greek yogurt, or 4 fried eggs**

1 Pour the lentils into a large bowl and add the boiling water; set aside.

2 Put the oil in the pot, select **SAUTÉ,** and adjust to **MORE/HIGH** heat. When the oil is hot, add the onion and cook, stirring occasionally, until well browned, 10 to 12 minutes. Add ¼ cup water and simmer until evaporated, scraping up any browned bits from the bottom of the pot, 30 seconds. Add the garlic and cumin to the pot and cook until fragrant, 30 seconds. Press **CANCEL**. Set aside ¼ cup of the onion mixture for garnish.

3 Drain the lentils and add them to the pot with the onion. Add 2 cups of the broth, 1¼ teaspoons salt, and several grinds of pepper. Place a tall trivet in the pot. Combine the rice, the remaining 1 cup broth, and a generous pinch of salt in a 7 × 3-inch round metal baking pan (see Helpful Equipment, page 18). Place the baking pan, uncovered, on the trivet. Lock on the lid, select the **PRESSURE COOK** function, and adjust to **HIGH** pressure for 4 minutes. Make sure the steam valve is in the "Sealing" position.

(recipe continues)

(continued from page 98)

4 When the cooking time is up, let the pressure come down naturally for 10 minutes and then quick-release the remaining pressure. Fluff the rice with a fork. Remove the trivet and gently stir the lentils and rice together. Garnish with the reserved fried onions and serve with yogurt or fried eggs.

Tasty Tip: Substitute ghee for the olive oil for richer flavor.

Tasty Tip: Got ground allspice? Add ½ teaspoon to the lentils along with the cumin.

JAPANESE VEGETABLE CURRY

· · · · · · · · · ·

Serves 4

ACTIVE TIME	FUNCTION	TOTAL TIME	RELEASE
10 minutes	Sauté, Pressure	25 minutes	Quick

If you've never tried Japanese curry mixes like Vermont Curry or S & B Golden Curry, you're missing out! The little blocks make deliciously thick, slightly sweet sauce that goes well with winter vegetables like onions, carrots, Yukon Gold potatoes, and winter squash. I include extra-firm tofu for protein here, but diced chicken thighs or thinly sliced beef or pork are also delicious. Serve with cooked udon noodles or steamed rice.

1 tablespoon canola oil

1 large onion, sliced through the root end

4 cubes (2⅝ ounces total) mild Japanese curry sauce mix

1 pound winter squash or Yukon Gold potatoes, peeled and cut into 1-inch chunks

2 large carrots, peeled and cut at an angle into 1-inch-thick slices

1 pound extra-firm tofu, cut into 1-inch cubes

Cooked udon noodles or steamed rice, for serving

1 Put the oil in the pot, select **SAUTÉ,** and adjust to **MORE/HIGH** heat. When the oil is hot, add the onions and cook, stirring frequently, until tender, 4 minutes. Press **CANCEL.**

2 Add the curry mix and 1½ cups water and break up the curry cubes with a wooden spoon. Add the squash and carrots and stir very gently to combine. Place the tofu cubes on top, but do not stir them in. Lock on the lid, select the **PRESSURE COOK** function, and adjust to **HIGH** pressure for 8 minutes. Make sure the steam valve is in the "Sealing" position.

3 When the cooking time is up, quick-release the pressure. Stir gently to combine the tofu and other ingredients without breaking up the tofu. Serve with hot noodles or rice.

Tasty Tip: Substitute cubed boneless, skinless chicken thighs or thinly sliced pork or beef for the tofu. The cooking time will be the same.

ONE POT FREEKEH ZA'ATAR BOWLS

....

Serves 4

ACTIVE TIME	FUNCTION	TOTAL TIME	RELEASE
10 minutes	Pressure	30 minutes	Quick

This Middle Eastern salad makes a great vegetarian lunchbox meal, or you can serve it as a side dish with grilled lamb chops or chicken. Freekeh (pronounced FREE-kah) are whole-grain wheat kernels that have been smoked or parched. They have an easy-to-love nutty flavor and tender texture that's perfect for grain bowls like this one. Za'atar is a zesty herb blend used in Middle Eastern cooking. Look for freekeh and za'atar at well-stocked supermarkets and online. If you can't find freekeh, substitute coarse bulgur and reduce the cooking time to 2 minutes.

1   medium eggplant, cut into 2-inch cubes

Salt

1¼ cups store-bought vegetable or chicken broth, or homemade (page 226 or 227)

¾   cup cracked freekeh (such as Bob's Red Mill Cracked Freekeh)

1   tablespoon za'atar

2   tablespoons extra-virgin olive oil

1   (15-ounce) can chickpeas, drained and rinsed, or 1½ cups cooked chickpeas (page 225)

1   cup cherry tomatoes, halved

1   tablespoon red wine vinegar

1   medium garlic clove, finely chopped and smashed with the side of a knife

Freshly ground black pepper

1 Toss the eggplant with 1 teaspoon salt and set aside for 10 minutes to draw out the bitter juices. Pat the eggplant dry with paper towels. Rinse briefly and pat dry with paper towels again.

2 Combine the broth, freekeh, za'atar, ½ teaspoon salt, and 1 tablespoon of the oil in the pot. Add the chickpeas and then layer the eggplant on top, but don't stir it into the broth mixture. Lock on the lid, select the **PRESSURE COOK** function, and adjust to **HIGH** pressure for 5 minutes. Make sure the steam valve is in the "Sealing" position.

3 When the cooking time is up, quick-release the pressure. Transfer the grain mixture to a large serving bowl. In a small bowl, whisk together the remaining 1 tablespoon oil with the tomatoes, vinegar, garlic, and several grinds of pepper. Gently toss the dressing with the grain mixture and serve warm or at room temperature.

INDIAN POTATO AND CAULIFLOWER CURRY

ONE POT

. . . .

Serves 4

ACTIVE TIME	FUNCTION	TOTAL TIME	RELEASE
10 minutes	Sauté, Pressure	30 minutes	Quick

This vegan entrée is so filling, you'll never miss the meat. The trick to cooking the cauliflower under pressure without it falling apart is to cut the florets into large chunks, cook them on top of the other vegetables, and then break them up into bite-size pieces before serving.

2 tablespoons safflower oil

1 tablespoon brown mustard seeds

1 medium yellow onion, chopped

1 tablespoon hot curry powder

1½ cups chopped ripe tomatoes

3 medium Yukon Gold potatoes (about 8 ounces), unpeeled, cut into 1-inch cubes

Salt and freshly ground black pepper

1 medium (1½-pound) cauliflower, cut into large (3-inch) florets, stalk and core discarded

1 Put the oil in the pot, select **SAUTÉ,** and adjust to **NORMAL/MEDIUM** heat. When the oil is hot, add the mustard seeds and cook until they have popped and turned gray, 1 minute. Add the onion and curry powder and cook, stirring frequently, until the onion is tender, 4 minutes. Add the tomatoes and cook until they break down a bit, about 2 minutes. Press **CANCEL.**

2 Add the potatoes, ½ cup water, 1 teaspoon salt, and several grinds of pepper and stir into the tomato mixture. Place the cauliflower florets on top of the potato mixture, but don't stir. Lock on the lid, select the **PRESSURE COOK** function, and adjust to **LOW** pressure for 2 minutes. Make sure the steam valve is in the "Sealing" position.

3 When the cooking time is up, quick-release the pressure. Pour the mixture into a large serving bowl and break up the cauliflower a bit with a spoon. Serve immediately.

Tasty Tip: Make sure your curry powder is fresh—the spices will go stale after about 4 months, so buy only what you need and replace it often for the brightest tasting curries.

Tasty Tip: If tomatoes are not in season, substitute 1 (10-ounce) can diced tomatoes with green chilies and their juice.

POULTRY & SEAFOOD

TERIYAKI WINGS

Serves 6 as an appetizer or snack, 4 as an entrée

ACTIVE TIME	FUNCTION	TOTAL TIME	RELEASE
10 minutes	Pressure, Sauté	35 minutes	Natural + quick

These fall-apart-tender wings are a great appetizer for game day, or serve them with cooked rice and steamed broccoli for a full meal; the recipe makes plenty of sauce for dipping or drizzling.

3 pounds "party" chicken wings (separated at the joints)

½ cup plus 2 tablespoons low-sodium soy sauce

Salt and freshly ground black pepper

⅓ cup packed brown sugar

2 tablespoons cider vinegar or rice vinegar

4 teaspoons finely chopped fresh ginger

4 medium garlic cloves, finely chopped

1 tablespoon cornstarch

Tasty Tip:
Add 1 tablespoon hot sauce to the marinade for spicy teriyaki wings.

1 Pour 1½ cups water into the pot and place a trivet or steamer basket inside. In a large bowl, toss the wings with 2 tablespoons of the soy sauce and season with salt and pepper. Place the wings on the trivet or steamer basket. Lock on the lid, select the **PRESSURE COOK** function, and adjust to **HIGH** for 5 minutes. Make sure the steam valve is in the "Sealing" position.

2 Preheat the broiler and move an oven rack so that it is 4 inches below the broiler element. Line a baking sheet with foil and spray it with cooking spray. When the cooking time is up, quick-release the pressure. Transfer the wings to the prepared baking sheet. Discard the cooking liquid and remove the trivet or steaming basket from the pot.

3 Add the remaining ½ cup soy sauce, the brown sugar, vinegar, ginger, and garlic to the pot. Select **SAUTÉ** and adjust to **NORMAL/MEDIUM** heat. Bring to a simmer and cook, stirring frequently, until the sugar has dissolved, 3 minutes. In a small bowl, mix the cornstarch with 1 tablespoon water. Add the cornstarch mixture to the pot and cook, stirring constantly, until the sauce has thickened, 1 minute. Spoon the sauce over the wings, turning them so both sides are covered. Broil the wings until browned and crispy on the edges, 3 minutes.

BARBECUE CHICKEN–STUFFED SWEET POTATOES

· · · · · · · · ·

Serves 4

ACTIVE TIME	FUNCTION	TOTAL TIME	RELEASE
10 minutes	Pressure	45 minutes	Natural + quick

This one-pot meal works by cooking the chicken thighs in barbecue sauce in the bottom of the Instant Pot while the sweet potatoes cook on a trivet set over the chicken. Be sure to use small sweet potatoes (about 6 to 8 ounces each) so they are cooked in the same amount of time as the chicken.

1 cup thin barbecue sauce (such as Stubb's Original Legendary Bar-B-Q Sauce)

1 pound boneless, skinless chicken thighs, fat trimmed

4 small (6- to 8-ounce) garnet yams or sweet potatoes, pricked with a fork

Salt and freshly ground black pepper

1 cup sour cream

2 green onions, thinly sliced

1 Combine the barbecue sauce and chicken in the pot. Place a tall trivet (see Helpful Equipment, page 18) over the chicken and arrange the sweet potatoes on top. Lock on the lid, select the **PRESSURE COOK** function, and adjust to **HIGH** pressure for 18 minutes. Make sure the steam valve is in the "Sealing" position.

2 When the cooking time is up, let the pressure come down naturally for 10 minutes and then quick-release the remaining pressure. Split the sweet potatoes open lengthwise, season with salt and pepper, and set aside. Remove the trivet from the pot. Pull the chicken into shreds with two forks, return it to the sauce, and stir to combine. (The sauce will have browned in places on the bottom of the pot; just scrape them up and stir into the sauce.)

3 Divide the chicken among the sweet potatoes; you may not need all of the sauce. Top with dollops of sour cream and a sprinkle of the green onions and serve.

INDIAN MAKHANI CHICKEN

· · · · · · · · · ·

Serves 4

ACTIVE TIME	FUNCTION	TOTAL TIME	RELEASE
10 minutes	Sauté, Pressure	30 minutes	Quick

Indian recipes often have a list of ingredients a mile long, but this butter chicken recipe is streamlined thanks to jarred Indian curry paste. Be sure to buy curry paste, not one of those watery curry marinades or "simmer sauces." A little curry paste goes a long way; store the remaining paste in the refrigerator for several weeks or freeze it in a zip-top bag for months and break off only what you need. Try adding a few tablespoons when cooking rice, use it in meat marinades, or add a little to melted butter for a memorable bowl of popcorn!

3 tablespoons butter or ghee, at room temperature

1 medium yellow onion, halved and sliced through the root end

1 (10-ounce) can Ro-Tel tomatoes with green chilies, with juice

2 tablespoons mild Indian curry paste (such as Patak's)

1½ pounds boneless, skinless chicken thighs, fat trimmed, cut into 2- to 3-inch pieces

2 tablespoons all-purpose flour

Salt and freshly ground black pepper

1 Put 1 tablespoon of the butter or ghee in the pot, select **SAUTÉ,** and adjust to **NORMAL/MEDIUM** heat. Add the onion and cook, stirring frequently, until browned, 6 minutes. Press **CANCEL.**

2 Add the tomatoes to the pot, stir, and scrape up any browned bits on the bottom of the pot. Add the curry paste and stir to combine. Nestle the chicken into the sauce. Lock on the lid, select the **PRESSURE COOK** function, and adjust to **HIGH** pressure for 8 minutes. Make sure the steam valve is in the "Sealing" position.

3 When the cooking time is up, quick-release the pressure. In a small bowl, mix the remaining 2 tablespoons butter or ghee with the flour until smooth. Select **SAUTÉ,** adjust to **NORMAL/ MEDIUM** heat, and add the flour mixture to the pot in two additions, stirring between additions, and cook until the sauce is thickened, 1 minute. Press **CANCEL.** Season with salt and pepper and serve.

Tasty Tip:
There may be a little browned sauce on the bottom of the pot at the end of cooking. Gently scrape it up and stir it into the sauce; it adds lots of flavor!

🍲 STUFFED CHICKEN PARMESAN

Serves 4

ACTIVE TIME	FUNCTION	TOTAL TIME	RELEASE
20 minutes	Pressure	45 minutes	Natural + quick

This is a sort of deconstructed chicken Parmesan—chicken breasts are stuffed with soft breadcrumbs, cheese, and zucchini instead of coating the outside of the meat with breading. Use a marinara sauce that's not too thick or it will scorch a bit and your Instant Pot might have trouble coming up to pressure. Serve the chicken by itself or on top of spaghetti.

1 slice sturdy sandwich bread, finely chopped

1 small (5-ounce) zucchini, grated

½ cup grated Italian cheese blend

1 teaspoon Italian seasoning

   Salt and freshly ground black pepper

4 medium (8-ounce) boneless, skinless chicken breasts

1 (24-ounce) jar thin marinara sauce (such as Rao's)

Tasty Tip:

If you'd like to sneak more veggies into this dish, opt for a marinara with garden vegetables; you'll need 3 cups.

1 In a medium bowl, combine the breadcrumbs, zucchini, cheese, and Italian seasoning. Season with salt and pepper. Cut a horizontal slit into each chicken breast to form a 5- to 6-inch-long pocket. Stuff the chicken breasts with the breadcrumb mixture. Season the chicken with salt and pepper.

2 Pour the sauce into the pot. Add ¼ cup water to the marinara jar, screw on the lid, and shake. Add the tomato-y water to the pot. Set a handled trivet in the pot and place the chicken breasts on the trivet. Lock on the lid, select the **PRESSURE COOK** function, and adjust to **LOW** pressure for 8 minutes. Make sure the steam valve is in the "Sealing" position.

3 When the cooking time is up, let the pressure come down naturally for 5 minutes and then quick-release the remaining pressure. Make sure the chicken is cooked through; an instant-read thermometer inserted into the thickest part of the largest piece of chicken should register at least 165°F. If the chicken isn't done, select **SAUTÉ** and adjust to **LESS/LOW** heat. Remove the trivet, nestle the chicken into the sauce, and simmer a few minutes more, uncovered, until the chicken is done. Press **CANCEL**.

4 Serve the chicken with the sauce.

FRENCH CIDER AND MUSTARD-BRAISED CHICKEN

· · · · · · · · · ·

Serves 4

ACTIVE TIME	FUNCTION	TOTAL TIME	RELEASE
20 minutes	Sauté, Pressure	50 minutes	Quick

Hard apple cider is a common cooking ingredient in Normandy, France, a region that produces some of the world's best cider. In this rich French dish, bone-in chicken thighs are sautéed with bacon and braised with cider and mushrooms. It's delicious served over cooked egg noodles.

2 slices thick-cut bacon, chopped

8 bone-in chicken thighs, skin removed and fat trimmed

Salt and freshly ground black pepper

4 cups quartered cremini mushrooms (8 ounces)

2 large shallots, thinly sliced (¾ cup)

1½ cups bottled hard apple cider (12 ounces)

2 tablespoons grainy mustard

1 Select **SAUTÉ** and adjust to **NORMAL/MEDIUM** heat. Add the bacon and cook, stirring occasionally, until the bacon is browned, 3 to 4 minutes. Transfer to a bowl with a slotted spoon; leave the drippings in the pot. Season the chicken all over with salt and pepper. Add half the chicken to the pot and cook until browned on one side, 3 minutes. Transfer to a plate. (This step adds flavor to the sauce. Do not brown the other chicken.)

2 Add the mushrooms and shallots to the pot and sauté until the shallots are tender, 3 minutes. Add the cider and mustard and bring to a simmer, scraping up any browned bits on the bottom of the pot. Press **CANCEL**.

3 Add all the chicken, any accumulated juices, and the bacon to the pot. Lock on the lid, select the **PRESSURE COOK** function, and adjust to **HIGH** pressure for 20 minutes. Make sure the steam valve is in the "Sealing" position. (Or you can **SLOW COOK** it—see page 118.)

(recipe continues)

(continued from page 117)

4 When the cooking time is up, quick-release the pressure. Remove the lid and transfer the chicken and vegetables to a serving dish with a slotted spoon. Cover with foil and set aside.

5 Select **SAUTÉ,** adjust to **MORE/HIGH** heat, and bring to a simmer. Using a ladle, skim any liquid fat that pools on top of the sauce and discard. Cook until the sauce is reduced by half, 5 minutes. Press **CANCEL**. Pour the sauce over the chicken and serve.

> **Slow Cook It:** In Step 3, select **SLOW COOK**, adjust to **NORMAL/MEDIUM** heat, and set for 7 to 8 hours. Lock on the lid set to "Venting," or use a pan lid that fits snugly on the pot (see Helpful Equipment, page 18). Proceed with the recipe as directed.

ONE POT CHICKEN PENNE PUTTANESCA

· · · · · · · · · ·

Serves 4

ACTIVE TIME	FUNCTION	TOTAL TIME	RELEASE
10 minutes	Sauté, Pressure	30 minutes	Quick

This zesty Southern Italian pasta dish is made with ingredients you probably already have kicking around in your pantry and takes just 30 minutes from start to finish. The recipe includes boneless chicken breasts, but you can substitute 12 ounces frozen shrimp or a fresh tuna steak instead. The pinch of red pepper flakes makes this a slightly spicy dish; add more if you like.

2 small (6- to 7-ounce) boneless, skinless chicken breasts

Salt and freshly ground black pepper

2 tablespoons olive oil

12 ounces dry penne pasta

2½ cups store-bought chicken or vegetable broth, or homemade (page 227 or 226)

1 (14.5-ounce) can diced tomatoes with Italian herbs, with juices

½ cup oil-cured black or Kalamata olives

4 oil-packed rolled anchovies with capers, plus 1 tablespoon oil from the jar

Pinch of red pepper flakes

1 Pat the chicken dry with paper towels. Season the chicken all over with salt and several grinds of pepper. Put the oil in the pot, select **SAUTÉ,** and adjust to **NORMAL/MEDIUM** heat. When the oil is hot, add the chicken and cook until golden brown on one side, 3 minutes. Press **CANCEL**.

2 Add the penne, broth, tomatoes, olives, anchovies and oil, red pepper flakes, and several grinds of pepper. Stir everything together and place the chicken breasts on top of the pasta mixture. Lock on the lid, select the **PRESSURE COOK** function, and adjust to **LOW** pressure for 6 minutes. Make sure the steam valve is in the "Sealing" position.

3 When the cooking time is up, quick-release the pressure. Transfer the chicken to a cutting board and chop it into bite-size pieces. Return the chicken to the pot and stir to combine. Loosely cover the pot with the lid and let stand for 5 minutes; the liquid will thicken upon standing.

Tasty Tip: The pasta mixture will look too watery at first, but it's amazing how much liquid the pasta absorbs from the time you open the pot to the time you sit down to eat.

ONE POT CHICKEN AND ITALIAN SAUSAGE RAGU WITH POLENTA

· · · · · · · · · ·

Serves 4

ACTIVE TIME	FUNCTION	TOTAL TIME	RELEASE
15 minutes	Sauté, Pressure	55 minutes	Natural + quick

This one-pot meal features a saucy ragu of Italian sausage, chicken, peppers, and marinara sauce served with creamy polenta that's cooked with the "pot in pot" method. Be sure to use a thin marinara sauce; thicker sauces won't provide enough moisture to build up steam in the pot.

2 tablespoons olive oil

8 **ounces bulk spicy Italian sausage**

1 **medium yellow onion, chopped**

1 **red or green bell pepper, chopped**

1 tablespoon balsamic vinegar

1 **cup thin marinara sauce (such as Rao's or Trader Joe's Organic Marinara)**

¼ cup store-bought chicken broth, or homemade (page 227)

12 **ounces boneless, skinless chicken thighs, fat trimmed, cut into 2-inch pieces**

1 Put 1 tablespoon of the oil in the pot, select **SAUTÉ**, and adjust to **NORMAL/MEDIUM** heat. Add the sausage and cook, stirring occasionally, until browned, 3 minutes (see Tasty Tip, opposite). Add the onion and bell pepper and cook until tender, 4 minutes. Press **CANCEL**.

2 Add the vinegar and scrape up the browned bits on the bottom of the pan. Add the marinara sauce and broth and stir to combine. Season the chicken all over with salt and pepper. Add it to the pot and stir to combine.

3 Place a tall trivet in the pot over the chicken. Place 2⅔ cups warm water, the remaining 1 tablespoon oil, and ½ teaspoon salt in a 7-inch round metal baking pan (see Helpful Equipment, page 18). Gradually whisk in the polenta. Cover tightly with foil and place on the trivet. Lock on the lid, select the **PRESSURE COOK** function, and adjust to **HIGH** pressure for 8 minutes. Make sure the steam valve is in the "Sealing" position.

Salt and freshly ground
black pepper

¾ **cup polenta (not quick-cooking)**

OPTIONAL GARNISH

½ cup shaved Parmesan cheese
curls (see Tasty Tip, below)

4 When the cooking time is up, let the pressure come down naturally for 10 minutes and then quick-release the remaining pressure. Remove the lid, and blot the top of the foil on the baking dish with a paper towel to remove any water. Carefully lift the baking dish out of the pot, remove the foil, and stir the polenta. (It will look thin at first, but it thickens after stirring.) Remove the trivet from the pot. Serve the polenta in shallow bowls, topped with the chicken ragu and garnished with the cheese curls, if desired.

Tasty Tip: To make curls of Parmesan cheese, use a sharp vegetable peeler to peel thin strips from a block of the cheese, avoiding the hard rind.

Tasty Tip: Fat content in sausages varies. If there's a lot of excess fat in the pot after browning the sausage in Step 1, pour off all but 1 tablespoon before proceeding with the recipe.

CHICKEN AND QUINOA BURRITO BOWLS

· · · · · · · · · · ·

Serves 4

ACTIVE TIME	FUNCTION	TOTAL TIME	RELEASE
15 minutes	Sauté, Pressure	40 minutes	Quick

Chicken thighs become fall-apart tender when braised in salsa in this easy recipe. Quinoa and beans are cooked using the "pot in pot" method, making it a great one-pot dinner. Serve garnished with any of the optional colorful toppings or fold the ingredients into tortillas for burritos.

2 **teaspoons taco seasoning (see Tasty Tip, opposite)**

6 **to 8 boneless, skinless chicken thighs, fat trimmed**

2 tablespoons olive oil

¾ **cup fresh refrigerated tomato salsa**

1 cup plus 1 tablespoon store-bought chicken broth, or homemade (page 227)

¾ **cup red quinoa, rinsed**

1 **(15-ounce) can black beans, drained and rinsed, or 1½ cups home-cooked beans (see page 225)**

Salt and freshly ground black pepper

1 **cup prepared guacamole**

1 Rub the taco seasoning into the chicken. Put the oil in the pot, select **SAUTÉ**, and adjust to **MORE/HIGH** heat. When the oil is hot, brown the chicken in batches on one side only until golden brown, 3 minutes per batch. Press **CANCEL**. Drain off the fat in the pot and return the pot to the appliance.

2 Add ½ cup of the salsa and ¼ cup of the broth to the pot and scrape up the browned bits on the bottom of the pot. Add the chicken and any accumulated juices to the pot. Spoon the remaining ¼ cup salsa over the chicken.

3 Place a tall trivet in the pot over the chicken. In a 7-inch metal baking pan, combine the quinoa and remaining ¾ cup plus 1 tablespoon broth. Spoon the beans over the quinoa mixture, but don't stir them in. Place the uncovered baking pan on the trivet. Lock on the lid, select the **PRESSURE COOK** function, and adjust to **HIGH** pressure for 12 minutes. Make sure the steam valve is in the "Sealing" position.

OPTIONAL TOPPINGS

Shredded cheddar cheese

Sour cream

Sliced olives

4 When the cooking time is up, quick-release the pressure. Remove the baking pan and trivet from the pot. Fluff the quinoa-bean mixture with a fork and season with salt and pepper. Divide the quinoa among bowls and top with the chicken and some of the cooking liquid from the pot. Top with the guacamole. Sprinkle with the optional toppings, if using, and serve.

Tasty Tip: Use clean kitchen scissors to trim off the fat on the chicken thighs; it will reduce the amount of fat in the sauce.

Tasty Tip: Be sure to use a taco seasoning that does not contain cornstarch or other thickeners to prevent scorching on the bottom of the pot. I like Simply Organic taco seasoning packets.

FAUX-TISSERIE ROASTED CHICKEN DINNER

·············

Serves 4 to 6

ACTIVE TIME	FUNCTION	TOTAL TIME	RELEASE
10 minutes	Pressure, Sauté (optional)	1 hour 5 minutes	Quick

This recipe yields a chicken every bit as juicy and tender as grocery store rotisserie birds. A quick trip under the broiler will give you crispy skin, but it's an optional step. For a one-pot meal, loosely stuff the cavity and area around the chicken with carrots and potatoes for an easy side dish. Be sure to buy a bird that is as close to 4 pounds as possible; larger chickens won't fit in the pot. The gravy is an optional step, but it takes just minutes to make in the same pot you cooked the chicken in, so go for it!

1 (4-pound) whole roasting chicken, neck and giblets in cavity removed and reserved

1 pound red potatoes, cut into 1¼-inch chunks

2 large carrots, peeled and cut into 1-inch pieces

2 tablespoons olive oil

4 teaspoons lemon pepper seasoning (not salt-free)

OPTIONAL GRAVY

1½ tablespoons all-purpose flour

1½ tablespoons butter, at room temperature

Salt and freshly ground black pepper

1 Place a trivet with handles in the pot and add 1 cup water. Place the neck and giblets, if you have them, in the water. Toss the vegetables with 1 tablespoon of the oil and 1 teaspoon of the lemon pepper seasoning. Stuff about half the potatoes and carrots into the chicken cavity; do not pack them in or they will not cook evenly. Tuck the wings behind the chicken's back and tie the drumsticks together with butcher's twine. Season the outside of the chicken with the remaining lemon pepper seasoning.

2 Place the chicken breast-side up on the trivet. Place the remaining carrots and potatoes around the chicken. Drizzle with the remaining 1 tablespoon oil. Lock on the lid, select the **PRESSURE COOK** function, and adjust to **HIGH** pressure for 28 minutes. Make sure the steam valve is in the "Sealing" position and that the "Keep Warm" button is off.

(recipe continues)

(continued from page 125)

3 When the cooking time is up, quick-release the pressure. An instant-read thermometer should read 160°F when inserted into the breast. If the chicken is not done, cover with a regular pot lid, select **SAUTÉ,** and adjust to **NORMAL/MEDIUM** for 5 minutes. Press **CANCEL.**

4 For crispy skin, preheat the broiler and adjust the oven rack so that it is 8 inches below the broiler element. Transfer the chicken on the trivet to a foil-lined baking sheet. Place the loose vegetables in a serving bowl and cover with foil. Broil the chicken, rotating the pan once, until the skin on top is browned, about 6 minutes. Carve the chicken and serve with the vegetables and a little of the cooking liquid.

5 If you'd like to make gravy, with the cooking liquid still in the pot, select **SAUTÉ** and adjust to **MORE/HIGH** heat. Liquid fat will pool around the edges of the pot as the liquid comes to a simmer. Use a ladle to skim off the fat; discard. In a small bowl, stir the butter and flour together until smooth. Whisk the flour mixture into the cooking liquid and simmer until thickened, 2 minutes. Press **CANCEL**. Serve with the chicken.

Tasty Tip: Add a splash of soy sauce to the gravy for a richer flavor and color.

QUINOA AND SAUSAGE-STUFFED PEPPERS

· · · · · · · · · ·

Serves 4

ACTIVE TIME	FUNCTION	TOTAL TIME	RELEASE
35 minutes	Sauté, Pressure	1 hour 5 minutes	Natural + quick

The earthy flavor of quinoa marries well with marinara and peppers in this modern spin on the classic comfort food. There's no need to cook the sausage before adding it to the stuffing; it will cook through and stay moist in 15 minutes under **HIGH** pressure.

⅔ cup dry quinoa, rinsed and drained

1¾ cups store-bought chicken broth, or homemade (page 227)

Salt and freshly ground black pepper

1 pound raw Italian chicken or turkey sausages, casings removed

½ cup chopped fresh basil

4 medium bell peppers, top ¼ inch of stem end removed, seeds discarded

1 cup thin jarred marinara sauce (such as Rao's)

1 cup grated mozzarella cheese

Tasty Tip: You can use precooked quinoa or rice instead of cooking it in Step 1, which will reduce the recipe's total time by about 40 minutes. Use 2 cups cooked quinoa or rice and reduce the broth in the recipe to ¾ cup.

1 Place the quinoa, 1 cup of the broth, a pinch of salt, and a few grinds of pepper in the pot. Lock on the lid, select the **PRESSURE COOK** function, and adjust to **HIGH** pressure for 1 minute. Make sure the steam valve is in the "Sealing" position. When the cooking time is up, let the pressure come down naturally for 10 minutes and then quick-release the remaining pressure. Pour the quinoa into a large bowl and fluff with a fork. Let it cool for 5 minutes. Rinse out the pot and return it to the appliance. (Alternatively, you can use precooked quinoa or rice; see Tasty Tip below.)

2 Add the sausage and basil to the quinoa and mix well to combine. Stuff the quinoa mixture into the peppers.

3 In a small bowl, combine the remaining ¾ cup broth with the marinara sauce. Pour 1¼ cups of the mixture into the pot. Place a trivet with handles in the pot and set the peppers on top. Spoon the remaining sauce over the peppers and sprinkle with the cheese. Lock on the lid, select the **PRESSURE COOK** function, and adjust to **HIGH** pressure for 15 minutes. Make sure the steam valve is in the "Sealing" position.

4 When the cooking time is up, let the pressure come down naturally for 10 minutes and then quick-release the remaining pressure. Carefully lift the trivet from the pot and transfer the peppers to dinner plates. Spoon the sauce over the peppers.

ONE POT CHICKEN WITH BLACK BEAN GARLIC SAUCE AND BROCCOLI

· · · · · · · · · ·

Serves 4

ACTIVE TIME	FUNCTION	TOTAL TIME	RELEASE
10 minutes	Pressure, Sauté	35 minutes	Quick

Black bean garlic sauce is a rich, savory Chinese condiment made from fermented black beans, garlic, and red peppers. Look for it in grocery stores where other Chinese condiments like oyster sauce are found.

1½ pounds boneless, skinless chicken thighs, fat trimmed, cut into 2-inch pieces

½ cup store-bought chicken broth, or homemade (page 227)

3 tablespoons black bean garlic sauce (such as Lee Kum Kee brand)

1½ tablespoons julienned fresh ginger

1 tablespoon soy sauce

1 teaspoon balsamic vinegar
  Freshly ground black pepper

1½ cups long-grain white rice, rinsed (optional)

4 cups 1½-inch broccoli florets (10 ounces)

2 teaspoons cornstarch

1 Combine the chicken, broth, black bean garlic sauce, ginger, soy sauce, and vinegar in the Instant Pot. Add several grinds of pepper.

2 If you'd like to serve the chicken with rice, combine the rice with 1½ cups cold water in a 7 × 3-inch round metal baking pan. Place the baking pan, uncovered, on a tall trivet set over the chicken mixture.

3 Lock on the lid, select the **PRESSURE COOK** function, and adjust to **HIGH** pressure for 5 minutes. Make sure the steam valve is in the "Sealing" position.

4 When the cooking time is up, quick-release the pressure. Remove the rice in the baking pan and the trivet, if you used them, and set aside. Add the broccoli to the pot, stir gently to combine, and place a regular pot lid on the Instant Pot. Select **SAUTÉ**, adjust to **NORMAL/MEDIUM** heat, and simmer until the broccoli is crisp-tender, 3 minutes.

5 While the mixture is cooking, mix the cornstarch with 2 teaspoons cold water. Add to the pot, stir, and continue to cook until the sauce is thickened, 30 seconds. Press **CANCEL**. Serve immediately with the rice.

GAME HENS WITH 40 CLOVES OF GARLIC

· · · · · · · · · ·

Serves 4

ACTIVE TIME	FUNCTION	TOTAL TIME	RELEASE
15 minutes	Sauté, Pressure	45 minutes	Natural + quick

Game hens are deliciously tender when cooked under pressure. Forty cloves of garlic may sound like a lot, but the cloves mellow considerably under pressure and dissolve into a deliciously rich sauce in the end. To save time, you can buy already peeled garlic cloves in the produce section of most grocery stores.

2 **(24-ounce) Cornish game hens**

1 **tablespoon olive oil**

2 **teaspoons herbes de Provence (see Tasty Tip, page 132)**

Salt and freshly ground black pepper

40 **medium garlic cloves (about ¾ cup), peeled**

¼ **cup dry white wine**

½ **cup store-bought chicken broth, or homemade (page 227)**

1½ **tablespoons all-purpose flour**

1 **tablespoon butter, at room temperature**

1 Place the hens breast-side down on a clean cutting board. Using kitchen shears, cut down the backbone of each bird. Cut lengthwise through the breastbone to cleave the birds in half. Add the oil to the pot, select **SAUTÉ**, and adjust to **MORE/HIGH** heat. Rub the hens all over with the herbes de Provence, salt, and pepper. When the oil is hot, brown the poultry skin-side down in batches until golden brown on one side, 4 minutes per batch. Transfer to a plate.

2 Adjust the heat to **NORMAL/MEDIUM**. Add the garlic and cook, stirring frequently, until fragrant and browned in places, 1 minute. Add the wine, scrape up any browned bits on the bottom of the pot, and simmer for 1 minute. Press **CANCEL**.

3 Add the broth and stir to combine. Place a trivet with handles in the pot. Place the hen halves skin-side up on the rack. You may have to stack them a bit, which is fine. Lock on the lid, select the **PRESSURE COOK** function, and adjust to **HIGH** pressure for 8 minutes. Make sure the steam valve is in the "Sealing" position.

(recipe continues)

(continued from page 131)

4 When the cooking time is up, let the pressure come down naturally for 10 minutes and then quick-release the remaining pressure. Carefully lift the trivet out of the pot with oven mitts, transfer the hens to a serving plate, and cover loosely with foil.

5 In a small bowl, mix the flour and butter until smooth. Select **SAUTÉ** and adjust to **NORMAL/MEDIUM** heat. Clear fat will pool around the edges of the pot as the liquid begins to simmer; use a ladle to skim this off and discard it. Whisk the flour mixture into the liquid in the pot in two additions and simmer until the sauce has thickened, 1 minute. Press **CANCEL**. Season the sauce with salt and pepper, spoon over the hens, and serve immediately.

Tasty Tip: Herbes de Provence is a French spice blend available at most grocery stores and in the bulk spice section of whole-foods markets. If you can't find it, blend equal parts dried thyme, marjoram, oregano, rosemary, savory, and a few pinches of dried lavender flowers, or use your own favorite herb seasoning blend.

Tasty Tip: You can use chicken legs instead of game hens, if you'd like. Increase the pressure cooking time in Step 3 to 13 minutes.

BRAISED CALAMARI IN TOMATO SAUCE

Serves 4

ACTIVE TIME	FUNCTION	TOTAL TIME	RELEASE
10 minutes	Sauté, Pressure	1 hour	Quick

This elegantly simple squid-tomato sauce is delicious served as a stew with warm sourdough bread or tossed with pasta. Look for cleaned, cut-up squid in the freezer section of well-stocked markets. The amount of liquid in this recipe may look scarce at first, but squid give off a lot of liquid as they cook.

2 tablespoons olive oil

1 medium yellow onion, chopped

4 medium garlic cloves, chopped

1 teaspoon dried oregano

¼ cup dry red wine

1 (14-ounce) can diced tomatoes with Italian herbs, with juice

1 pound frozen cleaned and sliced squid

Salt and freshly ground black pepper

OPTIONAL GARNISH

Lemon wedges

1 Put the oil in the pot, select **SAUTÉ**, and adjust to **NORMAL/MEDIUM** heat. When the oil is hot, add the onion and cook, stirring frequently, until beginning to brown, 6 minutes. Add the garlic and oregano and cook until fragrant, 45 seconds.

2 Add the wine and simmer for 1 minute, scraping up the browned bits on the bottom of the pot. Press **CANCEL**. Add the tomatoes, squid, and several grinds of pepper. Lock on the lid, select the **PRESSURE COOK** function, and adjust to **HIGH** pressure for 20 minutes. Make sure the steam valve is in the "Sealing" position.

3 When the cooking time is up, quick-release the pressure. Season with salt and pepper. Serve with lemon wedges, if desired.

Tasty Tip: If you can't find cut-up squid, buy whole squid tubes and tentacles and clean them yourself. Cut the tubes away from the head and tentacles. Remove the hard, clear quill inside the tubes and slice the tubes into 1-inch rings. Cut the eye portion away from the tentacles and discard. Remove the hard beaks from the center of the tentacle portion where the tentacles meet.

TURKEY PESTO MEATBALLS WITH PASTA

· · · · · · · · · ·

Serves 4

ACTIVE TIME	FUNCTION	TOTAL TIME	RELEASE
15 minutes	Pressure	40 minutes	Quick

These tender meatballs are cooked with short pasta twists called gemelli and prepared pesto for a unique spin on pasta and meatballs. Prepared pesto varies greatly in quality; be sure to buy fresh (not jarred) pesto that has basil and olive oil listed at the top of the ingredients list.

1 pound Italian turkey sausage, casings removed and discarded

¼ cup dry Italian breadcrumbs

1 large egg

12 ounces dry gemelli pasta, medium shells, or rotini

3 cups store-bought chicken broth, or homemade (page 227)

1 cup fresh prepared basil pesto (such as Buitoni)

Salt and freshly ground black pepper

1 cup fresh basil leaves, torn into small pieces

1 In a medium bowl, mix the sausage meat, breadcrumbs, and egg. Divide the mixture into 20 portions, about 1 heaping tablespoon each. Set aside.

2 Place the pasta, broth, pesto, 1 cup water, ½ teaspoon salt, and several grinds of pepper in the pot and stir to combine. Place the meatballs on top of the pasta mixture. Lock on the lid, select the **PRESSURE COOK** function, and adjust to **LOW** pressure for 5 minutes. Make sure the steam valve is in the "Sealing" position and that the "Keep Warm" button is off.

3 When the cooking time is up, quick-release the pressure. Gently stir the fresh basil into the pasta mixture and season with salt and pepper, taking care not to break up the meatballs.

TURKEY BREAST WITH STUFFING AND GRAVY

· · · · · · · · · ·

Serves 4

ACTIVE TIME	FUNCTION	TOTAL TIME	RELEASE
25 minutes	Sauté, Pressure	1 hour 20 minutes	Natural + quick

Turkey breast is exceptionally juicy when cooked in the moist environment of the Instant Pot. Use either a boneless turkey breast half with skin or a convenient tied turkey breast roast from the butcher case for this recipe. The stuffing is cooked in a metal baking pan or foil packet balanced on top of the turkey, for a one-pot Thanksgiving meal anytime.

5 tablespoons unsalted butter

1 small yellow onion, chopped

2 celery ribs, chopped

4 cups dry sage stuffing mix (such as Pepperidge Farm; 7 ounces)

2¾ cups store-bought chicken broth, or homemade (page 227)

1 (2½- to 2¾-pound) boneless, skin-on turkey breast half or tied turkey breast roast

Salt and freshly ground black pepper

1 tablespoon olive oil

2½ tablespoons all-purpose flour

1 Smear 1 tablespoon of the butter in a 7 × 3-inch round metal baking pan (4- to 6-cup; see Helpful Equipment, page 18) or butter the center of a 12-inch length of foil.

2 Put 1 tablespoon of the butter in the pot, select **SAUTÉ**, and adjust to **NORMAL/MEDIUM** heat. When the butter has melted, add the onion and celery and cook, stirring frequently, until tender, 4 minutes. Press **CANCEL**. Pour the vegetables into a bowl, add the stuffing mix and 1¼ cups of the broth, and stir to moisten. Pour into the prepared baking pan and cover tightly with foil. If using foil instead of a baking pan, pour the stuffing into the center of the foil and bring the edges up to create a packet; set aside.

3 Season the turkey breast all over with salt and pepper and drizzle with the oil. Select **SAUTÉ** and adjust to **NORMAL/MEDIUM** heat. When the pot is hot, place the turkey breast skin-side down in the pot and cook until golden brown, 3 minutes. Press **CANCEL**. Remove the turkey breast from the pot.

(recipe continues)

(continued from page 137)

4 Add the remaining 1½ cups broth to the pot and scrape up any browned bits on the bottom.

5 Place a trivet with handles into the pot and place the turkey breast skin-side up on the trivet. Place the stuffing in the baking pan or foil packet on top of the turkey breast. Lock on the lid, select the **PRESSURE COOK** function, and adjust to **HIGH** pressure for 35 minutes. Make sure the steam valve is in the "Sealing" position.

6 When the cooking time is up, let the pressure come down naturally for 10 minutes. Quick-release any remaining pressure. Remove the stuffing pan from the pot.

7 Insert an instant-read thermometer into the thickest part of the breast; it should read 160°F. If it doesn't, cover the pot with a regular pot lid, select **SAUTÉ**, adjust to **LESS/LOW** heat, and simmer briefly until 160°F is reached. Press **CANCEL**. Transfer the turkey breast to a cutting board and cover loosely with foil; leave the cooking liquid in the pot.

8 In a medium bowl, combine the remaining 3 tablespoons butter with the flour and stir until smooth. Select **SAUTÉ** and adjust to **NORMAL/MEDIUM** heat. Gradually whisk the flour mixture into the cooking liquid and cook until bubbly, 3 minutes. Season with salt and pepper. Press **CANCEL**.

9 Slice the turkey roast crosswise. Serve with the gravy and stuffing.

Tasty Tip:

If you want crispy stuffing, broil it 4 inches below the broiler element until lightly browned, 2 to 3 minutes. If you used a foil packet, transfer the stuffing to a baking dish before broiling.

SALMON WITH CITRUS BUTTER SAUCE

· · · · · · · · · ·

Serves 4

ACTIVE TIME	FUNCTION	TOTAL TIME	RELEASE
10 minutes	Pressure, Sauté	28 minutes	Natural + quick

Thick, center-cut salmon fillets remain moist when bathed in flavorful steam under low pressure. The steaming liquid, a mix of dry white wine and citrus juice, is the base for the elegant French butter sauce called beurre blanc. Serve the salmon on plain rice with steamed broccoli on the side.

½ cup dry white wine

¼ cup fresh orange juice (about ½ large navel orange)

2 tablespoons fresh lime juice

1 tablespoon finely chopped shallots

4 (5-ounce) skin-on center-cut wild salmon fillet portions, pin bones removed

   Salt and freshly ground black pepper

8 tablespoons (1 stick) cold, unsalted butter, cut into ¼-inch dice and refrigerated

1 Combine the wine, orange juice, lime juice, and shallot in the pot. Place a trivet with handles in the pot. Season the fleshy side of the salmon with salt and pepper and place the fillets skin-side down on the trivet. (You may need to tuck the thin end of the fillets under so all the pieces fit.)

2 Lock on the lid, select the **PRESSURE COOK** function, and adjust to **LOW** pressure for 1 minute. Make sure the steam valve is in the "Sealing" position.

3 When the cooking time is up, let the pressure come down naturally for 5 minutes and then quick-release the remaining pressure. Lift the trivet with the salmon on it from the pot, transfer the salmon to a serving platter, and cover loosely with foil.

4 Select **SAUTÉ** and adjust to **MORE/HIGH** heat. Simmer the cooking liquid until it is syrupy and has reduced by half, about 8 minutes. Press **CANCEL**. Remove the pot from the Instant Pot. Gradually whisk in about 2 tablespoons of the cold butter. Return the pot to the appliance and continue to

(recipe continues)

(continued from page 139)

gradually whisk in the butter with the power off. Add more butter only after the last addition has melted. If the sauce begins to look oily, it's getting too warm; remove the pot from the appliance and continue to whisk in the butter. Season the sauce with salt. Immediately serve the salmon blanketed with the sauce.

Tasty Tip: To judge the doneness of fish, insert a small knife into the thickest part of a fillet, count to three, and then carefully touch the dull side of the knife to your bottom lip. If the knife is cold, the fish is rare in the center. If the knife is warm, the fish is cooked correctly. If the knife is very hot, the fish will be a bit overdone.

🍲 FISH WITH GINGER AND ASPARAGUS

Serves 4

ACTIVE TIME	FUNCTION	TOTAL TIME	RELEASE
5 minutes	Pressure, Sauté	15 minutes	Quick

For this recipe, use firm, white-fleshed fish like ling cod or halibut in fillets that are at least 1 inch thick to prevent the fish from overcooking. The asparagus is cooked in a partially sealed foil packet to protect it from overcooking. Since asparagus spears vary in size, this recipe includes instructions for cooking them further, if necessary.

2 tablespoons soy sauce

1 tablespoon rice vinegar or cider vinegar

1 tablespoon toasted sesame oil

1 teaspoon sugar

4 (6-ounce) ling cod or halibut fillet portions, 1 inch thick, skin removed

Salt and freshly ground black pepper

1 (2-inch) piece fresh ginger, peeled and cut into julienned strips (about ¼ cup)

1 pound asparagus (ideally ½-inch-thick stalks), tough ends snapped off and discarded

1 Place a steaming basket in the pot and add 1 cup warm water. In a small measuring cup, combine the soy sauce, vinegar, sesame oil, and sugar and stir to dissolve the sugar.

2 Drizzle the fish with 4 teaspoons of the soy sauce mixture and season with salt and a few grinds of pepper. Place the fish on the steaming basket. Sprinkle the ginger over the fish. Place the asparagus on a 12-inch piece of foil, brush with a little of the soy sauce mixture, and season with salt and pepper. Bring up the sides of the foil to encase the asparagus, leaving a 2-inch-wide opening at the top. Poke a few holes in the bottom of the foil packet to let the steam circulate. Place the packet on top of the fish.

3 Lock on the lid, select the **PRESSURE COOK** function, and adjust to **LOW** pressure for 2 minutes. Make sure the steam valve is in the "Sealing" position.

4 When the cooking time is up, quick-release the pressure. Carefully lift the foil packet and steaming basket out of the pot. Transfer the fish and ginger to a large serving plate. If the asparagus is not done to your liking, return the steaming basket to the pot, remove the foil, and place the asparagus on the steaming basket. Select **SAUTÉ**, adjust to **MORE/HIGH** heat, cover with the lid, and adjust the vent to "Venting." Cook, checking frequently, until the asparagus is done to your liking. (This should take no more than 3 minutes for very thick asparagus.) Arrange the asparagus around the fish on the platter and drizzle with the remaining soy sauce mixture. Serve immediately.

Tasty Tip: Season the steaming water with the ginger trimmings and a few garlic cloves, if desired. The aromatic steam will subtly infuse the fish with flavor.

ONE POT SHRIMP PAELLA

Serves 4

ACTIVE TIME	FUNCTION	TOTAL TIME	RELEASE
10 minutes	Sauté, Pressure	45 minutes	Natural + quick

This one-pot dinner features the flavors of sunny Spain—onions, red bell peppers, shrimp, and rice all cooked in a golden saffron-infused broth. Look for large or jumbo-size "easy-peel" shrimp (the veins will have been removed, but the shell will still be on) in the freezer section of grocery stores and big box stores. The shells protect the shrimp from overcooking and add lots of flavor to the broth. If you can't find "easy-peel" shrimp, use frozen peeled shrimp.

1¾ cups store-bought chicken or vegetable broth, or homemade (page 227 or 226)

2 **big pinches of saffron**

3 tablespoons olive oil

1 **medium yellow onion, chopped**

1½ **cups long-grain rice**

1 **cup drained canned fire-roasted tomatoes with garlic**

1 **cup drained, chopped roasted bell peppers**

Salt and freshly ground black pepper

1 **pound frozen large/jumbo shell-on, deveined shrimp**

OPTIONAL GARNISH

Lemon wedges

1 In a measuring cup, combine the broth and saffron and set aside. Put the oil in the pot, select **SAUTÉ,** and adjust to **MORE/HIGH** heat. When the oil is hot, add the onion and cook, stirring frequently, until tender, 4 minutes. Add the rice and stir to coat with the oil. Press **CANCEL**.

2 Add the broth with saffron, the tomatoes, roasted peppers, ¾ teaspoon salt, and several grinds of pepper and stir to combine. Place the frozen shrimp on top of the rice mixture, but do not stir them in. Lock on the lid, select the **PRESSURE COOK** function, and adjust to **MORE/HIGH** pressure for 4 minutes. Make sure the steam valve is in the "Sealing" position.

3 When the cooking time is up, let the pressure come down naturally for 10 minutes and then quick-release the remaining pressure. Gently pour the paella into a serving dish—don't stir too briskly or the rice will break up and become mushy. Serve immediately with lemon wedges on the side, if desired.

Tasty Tip: Add ½ cup sliced, cured Spanish chorizo (3 ounces) along with the rice in Step 1 for a smoky, meaty kick.

SHRIMP LINGUINI WITH SPINACH PESTO

· · · · · · · · · ·

Serves 4

ACTIVE TIME	FUNCTION	TOTAL TIME	RELEASE
15 minutes	Pressure	45 minutes	Quick

Raw shrimp tend to overcook in the Instant Pot, but frozen shrimp cook perfectly in 5 minutes on low pressure, which happens to be the exact time needed to cook linguini. In winter, I use baby spinach greens to make this pesto, but in summer, when basil is in season, I use a 50–50 mix of basil and spinach.

12 ounces linguini, broken in half

⅓ cup olive oil

4 medium garlic cloves

1½ cups store-bought vegetable or chicken broth, or homemade (page 226 or 227)

Salt and freshly ground black pepper

1¼ pounds large (16/20 count) frozen peeled and deveined shrimp

3 cups baby spinach or fresh basil leaves

⅓ cup pine nuts, toasted

Finely grated zest and juice of ½ lemon

Tasty Tip: Pine nuts can be costly; you can use toasted walnuts instead.

1 Put the linguini, 1 tablespoon of the oil, and 1 tablespoon of the garlic in the pot and toss to coat the pasta (this will keep the pasta from clumping). Add the broth, 1¼ cups hot water, ½ teaspoon salt, and several grinds of pepper and stir to combine, making sure most of the pasta is submerged. Place the frozen shrimp on top of the pasta mixture, but don't stir. Lock on the lid, select the **PRESSURE COOK** function, and adjust to **LOW** pressure for 5 minutes. Make sure the steam valve is in the "Sealing" position.

2 While the pasta is cooking, make the pesto. In a food processor or blender, blend the spinach or basil, the remaining olive oil, remaining garlic, 2 tablespoons of the pine nuts, the lemon zest, lemon juice, ½ teaspoon salt, and ¼ teaspoon pepper until combined.

3 When the cooking time is up, quick-release the pressure. Remove the lid and add the pesto. Stir with tongs, cover with the lid set to the "Venting" position, and allow the pasta to stand in the pot for 5 minutes. Don't skip this step—the pasta will finish cooking and absorb more of the sauce as it stands. Season with salt and pepper and serve garnished with the remaining pine nuts.

BEEF, PORK & LAMB

🏠 BEEFY TACO PASTA

·· ········ ··

Serves 4

ACTIVE TIME	FUNCTION	TOTAL TIME	RELEASE
10 minutes	Sauté, Pressure	35 minutes	Quick

This family-friendly pasta is reminiscent of the ground beef helper meals many of us grew up with, only better because it's homemade. Use very lean ground beef in this recipe so you don't have to take the extra step of draining off the drippings once the meat is browned. Be sure to use taco seasoning that does not contain cornstarch or other thickeners, such as Simply Organic Southwestern Taco Seasoning.

1 tablespoon olive oil

1 **pound 95% lean ground beef**

1 **medium yellow onion, chopped**

1 **(1.3-ounce) packet taco seasoning**

12 **ounces (dried/uncooked) short, chunky twisted pasta such as campanelle or gigli**

¼ **cup tomato paste**

1 **large red bell pepper, chopped**

Salt and freshly ground black pepper

OPTIONAL GARNISH

1 cup grated Cotija or pepper Jack cheese

1 Put the oil in the pot, select **SAUTÉ**, and adjust to **NORMAL/MEDIUM** heat. When the oil is hot, add the beef, onion, and 1 tablespoon of the taco seasoning and cook, breaking the meat into ½-inch chunks and stirring frequently, until the onion is tender (the beef will finish cooking under pressure), 6 minutes. Press **CANCEL**.

2 Add the pasta and stir to coat with the onions and beef. In a medium bowl or large measuring cup, whisk together 3 cups water, the tomato paste, and the remaining taco seasoning. Pour the mixture over the pasta in the pot and stir gently to combine. Place the bell pepper on top of the pasta mixture. Lock on the lid, select the **PRESSURE COOK** function, and adjust to **LOW** pressure for 5 minutes. Make sure the steam valve is in the "Sealing" position.

3 When the cooking time is up, quick-release the pressure. Gently stir the pasta with a rubber spatula, scraping any browned bits on the bottom of the pot. Season with salt and pepper. The sauce will thicken upon standing. Serve sprinkled with the optional cheese, if desired.

ONE POT # CALIFORNIA POT ROAST

· · · · · · · · · ·

Serves 4

ACTIVE TIME	FUNCTION	TOTAL TIME	RELEASE
30 minutes	Sauté, Pressure OR Slow Cook	2½ hours	Natural + quick

Braised in fruity Zinfandel wine and served with carrots and blue cheese mashed potatoes, this is the perfect one-pot Sunday supper. Be sure to buy a wine that you would drink yourself—½ cup of it is for the dish, the rest is for the chef!

1 **(3-pound) cross-rib chuck roast, cut into 3 large pieces**

Salt and freshly ground black pepper

2 tablespoons olive oil

1 **large yellow onion, sliced through the root end**

½ **cup Zinfandel wine**

½ cup store-bought beef broth, or homemade (page 228)

2 **large carrots, cut into 1½-inch lengths**

2 **pounds large Yukon Gold potatoes (about 5), peeled**

¼ **cup crumbled Gorgonzola dolce cheese, at room temperature**

1 Select **SAUTÉ** and adjust to **MORE/HIGH** heat. Season the meat liberally with salt and pepper and drizzle with the oil. When the pot is hot, add the roast and cook until browned on one side, 4 minutes. Transfer to a plate.

2 Add the onion to the pot and cook, stirring frequently, until tender, 4 minutes. Add the wine and simmer, scraping up the browned bits on the bottom of the pot, for 1 minute. Press **CANCEL**.

3 Return the roast to the pot browned-side down with any accumulated juices on the plate. Add the broth and arrange the carrots on top. Place a steamer basket on top of the beef and set the potatoes in the basket. Lock on the lid, select the **PRESSURE COOK** function, and adjust to **HIGH** for 1½ hours. Make sure the steam valve is in the "Sealing" position. (Or you can **SLOW COOK** it—see page 154.)

4 When the cooking time is up, let the pressure come down naturally for 15 minutes and then quick-release the remaining pressure.

(recipe continues)

(continued from page 153)

5 Transfer all but one of the potatoes to a serving bowl; the one in the pot will thicken the sauce. Mash the potatoes in the bowl with the cheese until smooth. Season with salt and pepper, cover, and set aside. Transfer most of the carrots and the meat to a serving platter; cover with foil.

6 Select **SAUTÉ** and adjust to **MORE/HIGH** heat. Simmer the cooking liquid until it is reduced by about half, 10 minutes. Using a ladle, skim off the liquid fat that pools around the edges of the pot and discard. Blend the sauce with an immersion blender or potato masher to break up the vegetables. Season with salt and pepper. Press **CANCEL**. Slice or shred the roast into thick slices and serve with the carrots, mashed potatoes, and sauce.

Slow Cook It: If using the **SLOW COOK** function, in Step 3 select **SLOW COOK**, adjust to **NORMAL/MEDIUM** heat, and set for 9 hours. Lock on the lid set to "Venting," or use a pan lid that fits snugly on the pot (see Helpful Equipment, page 18). Proceed with Step 5.

SWEET AND SAVORY BEEF BRISKET

. . . .

Serves 4 to 6

ACTIVE TIME	FUNCTION	TOTAL TIME	RELEASE
20 minutes	Sauté, Pressure OR Slow	2½ hours	Natural + quick

This brisket recipe makes a fork-tender roast in about half the time it takes in the oven. The sauce includes crushed tomatoes and vinegar for a sour component and onion and brown sugar for a bit of sweetness. Serve with the creamy Creamy Mashed Potatoes with Kale on page 214 or roasted Brussels sprouts in winter or coleslaw in the summer.

3 pounds beef brisket, fat cap trimmed to ¼ inch

1 tablespoon olive oil, plus more for drizzling the meat

Salt and freshly ground black pepper

1 large onion, sliced through the root end

1 tablespoon chopped fresh rosemary

1 cup crushed tomatoes with basil and garlic

½ cup store-bought beef broth, or homemade (page 228)

2 tablespoons packed brown sugar

2 tablespoons red wine vinegar

3 large carrots, peeled and left whole

1 Select **SAUTÉ** and adjust to **MORE/HIGH** heat. Drizzle the meaty side of the brisket with oil and season liberally all over with salt and pepper. When the pot is hot, add the brisket meaty-side down and cook until browned on that side, 4 minutes. Transfer to a plate.

2 Add the oil to the pot. When the oil is hot, add the onion and rosemary and cook, stirring frequently, until the onion begins to brown, 5 minutes. Press **CANCEL**. Add the tomatoes, broth, brown sugar, and vinegar and stir to combine.

3 Return the brisket to the pot fat-side up with any accumulated juices on the plate. Place the carrots on top of the brisket. Lock on the lid, select the **PRESSURE COOK** function, and adjust to **HIGH** for 1 hour 30 minutes. Make sure the steam valve is in the "Sealing" position. (Or you can **SLOW COOK** it—see page 156.)

(recipe continues)

(continued from page 155)

4 When the cooking time is up, let the pressure come down naturally for 25 minutes and then quick-release any remaining pressure (if pressure cooking).

5 Transfer the brisket and carrots to a cutting board and cover loosely with foil. Select **SAUTÉ** and adjust to **MORE/HIGH**. Simmer the cooking liquid until it is reduced by about half, about 10 minutes. Liquid fat will pool around the edges of the pot while it's simmering; use a ladle to skim this off and discard. Season with salt and pepper. Press **CANCEL**.

6 Thinly slice the brisket against the grain and cut the carrots into bite-size pieces, and serve with the sauce.

> ## Slow Cook It: Increase the broth to 1½ cups, the brown sugar to ¼ cup, and the vinegar to ⅓ cup, in order to submerge the meat; cut the carrots into 1½-inch pieces. In Step 3, select **SLOW COOK**, adjust to **NORMAL/MEDIUM** heat, and set for 10 to 11 hours. Lock on the lid set to "Venting," or use a pan lid that fits snugly on the pot (see Helpful Equipment, page 18). In Step 5, discard half of the cooking liquid before reducing the rest.

ITALIAN MEAT SAUCE

....

Serves 6

ACTIVE TIME	FUNCTION	TOTAL TIME	RELEASE
15 minutes	Sauté, Pressure	35 minutes	Quick

Cooking under pressure makes this quick pasta sauce taste like it's been simmering for hours. Using lean ground beef means you don't have to take an extra step to drain off the drippings, and browning the beef and onions together further expedites things. Serve this chunky sauce over your favorite pasta or on top of Creamy or Crispy Parmesan Polenta (page 211).

1 tablespoon olive oil

1 pound 95% lean ground chuck

1 medium yellow onion, chopped

3 tablespoons tomato paste

3 medium garlic cloves, chopped

2 teaspoons Italian seasoning

1 (28-ounce) can San Marzano–style tomatoes, chopped, with juice

½ cup store-bought beef broth, or homemade (page 228)

Salt and freshly ground black pepper

1 Put the oil in the pot, select **SAUTÉ**, and adjust to **MORE/HIGH** heat. When the oil is hot, add the ground beef and onion and cook, stirring frequently, until the meat is cooked and the onion is tender, 8 minutes. Leave some of the beef in large chunks for the best texture.

2 Push the meat and onion mixture to one side of the pot. Add the tomato paste, garlic, and Italian seasoning to the other side of the pot and cook until fragrant, 1 minute. Press **CANCEL**.

3 Add the tomatoes and the broth to the pot. Lock on the lid, select the **PRESSURE COOK** function, and adjust to **HIGH** pressure for 10 minutes. Make sure the steam valve is in the "Sealing" position.

4 When the cooking time is up, quick-release the pressure. Season the sauce with salt and pepper and serve.

Tasty Tip: For mushroom meat sauce, add 1½ cups quartered cremini mushrooms (6 ounces) and a pinch of salt to the pot along with the beef and onion and sauté until the mushrooms break down and release some of their liquid, 12 to 15 minutes.

BEEF STROGANOFF

· · · · · · · · · ·

Serves 4

ACTIVE TIME	FUNCTION	TOTAL TIME	RELEASE
15 minutes	Sauté, Pressure	50 minutes	Natural + quick

There are two roads to take with this recipe: Use tenderloin steak, as the namesake royal Russian family would have, or opt for thriftier sirloin or boneless short ribs and cook the dish for a bit longer. Dried porcini mushrooms add a ton of flavor to the sauce—don't be tempted to substitute bland fresh white mushrooms. Serve with egg noodles or rice.

2 **pounds beef tenderloin steak, sirloin steak, or boneless short ribs, fat trimmed**

Salt and freshly ground black pepper

2 tablespoons olive oil

1 **medium onion, finely chopped**

1 cup plus 2 tablespoons store-bought beef broth, or homemade (page 228)

½ **cup dried porcini or mixed wild mushrooms (½ ounce), rinsed to remove any grit**

1 **tablespoon Worcestershire sauce**

2 **tablespoons all-purpose flour**

½ **cup cultured sour cream (see Tasty Tip, opposite)**

OPTIONAL GARNISH

¼ cup chopped fresh dill

1 Select **SAUTÉ** and adjust to **MORE/HIGH** heat. Season the steaks with salt and pepper and drizzle with 1 tablespoon of the oil. When the pot is hot, add the steak in batches and cook until browned on both sides, 6 minutes per batch. Transfer the meat to a cutting board. Press **CANCEL.**

2 Select **SAUTÉ** and adjust to **NORMAL/MEDIUM** heat. Put the remaining 1 tablespoon oil in the pot, add the onion, and cook until tender, 3 minutes. While the onion cooks, use a fork and knife to cut the seared steaks into 1-inch pieces, returning the meat to the pot as you work. Press **CANCEL**.

3 Add 1 cup of the broth, the dried mushrooms, and the Worcestershire sauce to the pot and scrape up the browned bits on the bottom of the pot. Lock on the lid, select the **PRESSURE COOK** function, and adjust to **HIGH** pressure for 10 minutes if using tenderloin, 20 minutes if using sirloin or boneless short ribs. Make sure the steam valve is in the "Sealing" position.

4 When the cooking time is up, let the pressure come down naturally for 10 minutes and then quick-release the remaining pressure. Place the flour in a small bowl and gradually whisk in the remaining 2 tablespoons broth. Add the mixture to the pot, select **SAUTÉ**, and adjust to **NORMAL/MEDIUM** heat. Simmer, stirring very gently, until the sauce has thickened, 1 minute. Press **CANCEL**. Remove the pot from the appliance. Stir in the sour cream and season with salt and pepper. Stir in the dill, if desired. Serve with noodles or rice, if desired.

Tasty Tip: Cultured sour cream has a rich flavor and a thick texture and is less likely to curdle when stirred into hot liquid. Cultured sour cream is usually labeled as such. When in doubt, check the label: Real cultured sour cream won't contain guar gum and other stabilizers to thicken it.

SMOKY SHREDDED BEEF TACOS

· · · · · · · · · ·

Serves 4

ACTIVE TIME	FUNCTION	TOTAL TIME	RELEASE
20 minutes	Sauté, Pressure	1 hour 20 minutes	Natural + quick

Fall-apart-tender beef braised in a slightly spicy tomato-chipotle mixture makes a great filling for taco Tuesdays. If you can't find Ro-Tel tomatoes, substitute another brand of diced tomatoes with green chilies. You'll only need 1 chipotle pepper (about 1 tablespoon chopped); freeze the remainder in a zip-top freezer bag for up to 3 months.

1 tablespoon olive oil

2¼ **pounds beef chuck roast, cut into 6 large pieces**

Salt and freshly ground black pepper

⅓ cup store-bought beef broth, or homemade (page 228)

1 **(10-ounce) can Ro-Tel tomatoes, with juice**

3 **medium garlic cloves, chopped**

1 **chipotle pepper in adobo, chopped**

1 **tablespoon ground cumin**

8 **(6-inch) flour tortillas, warmed (see Tasty Tip, page 162)**

OPTIONAL GARNISHES

Guacamole

Shredded cheddar cheese

Shredded romaine lettuce

1 Select **SAUTÉ**, adjust to **MORE/HIGH** heat, and add the oil. Season the beef liberally with salt and pepper. When the pot is hot, add the meat and cook until browned all over, about 8 minutes. (Don't overcrowd the meat; you may want to do this in batches.) Transfer to a plate. Press **CANCEL**.

2 Add the broth and cook, scraping up any browned bits on the bottom of the pot. Add the tomatoes, garlic, chipotle pepper, and cumin and stir to combine. Return the meat and any accumulated juices to the pot and turn the meat in the tomato mixture to coat. Lock on the lid, select the **PRESSURE COOK** function, and adjust to **HIGH** for 35 minutes. Make sure the steam valve is in the "Sealing" position. (Or you can **SLOW COOK** it—see page 162.)

3 When the cooking time is up, let the pressure come down naturally for 20 minutes and then quick-release the remaining pressure. Transfer the meat to a cutting board and shred or chop it, discarding the fat and connective tissue. Put the beef in a large serving bowl. Use a slotted spoon to retrieve the tomatoes and garlic from the cooking liquid; add them to the beef. Cover.

(recipe continues)

(continued from page 161)

Tasty Tip: To warm flour tortillas, wrap them in moist paper towels and microwave them for 30 to 45 seconds; they'll become warm and pliable in the moist heat.

4 If you'd like to serve the beef with the cooking liquid, select **SAUTÉ** and adjust to **MORE/HIGH**. Simmer the cooking liquid until it is reduced by about half, about 10 minutes. Liquid fat will pool around the edges of the pot while it's simmering; use a ladle to skim this off and discard it. Press **CANCEL**. If you don't want to take this extra step, just spoon a few tablespoons of the liquid over the beef to moisten it and discard the remaining liquid. Serve the beef with the tortillas and optional garnishes.

Slow Cook It: Increase the broth to 1 cup, use 2 chipotle peppers, and substitute cumin seeds for the ground cumin. In Step 3, select **SLOW COOK**, adjust to **NORMAL/MEDIUM** heat, and set for 9 to 10 hours. Lock on the lid set to "Venting," or use a pan lid that fits snugly on the pot (see Helpful Equipment, page 18).

BRATWURST WITH SAUERKRAUT AND CIDER

· · · · · · · · · ·
Serves 4

ACTIVE TIME	FUNCTION	TOTAL TIME	RELEASE
10 minutes	Sauté, Pressure	40 minutes	Natural + quick

Serve this simple German-inspired meal with German Potato Salad (page 205), or mound the sausages on sturdy hoagie buns and top with the sauerkraut mixture, leaving behind the cider cooking liquid.

1 tablespoon olive oil

1 medium yellow onion, thinly sliced through the root end

1 teaspoon caraway seeds

1 (12-ounce) bottle dry, hard apple cider

1 (16-ounce) package refrigerated sauerkraut, drained

1 large Honeycrisp or Fuji apple, peeled, cored, and cut into 1-inch-thick wedges

1 pound smoked bratwurst or kielbasa sausages, left whole

Mustard, for serving (optional)

1 Put the oil in the pot, select **SAUTÉ**, and adjust to **NORMAL/MEDIUM** heat. When the oil is hot, add the onion and caraway seeds and cook until beginning to brown, 6 minutes. Add the cider and cook for 1 minute, scraping up the browned bits on the bottom of pot. Press **CANCEL**.

2 Add the sauerkraut and apple to the pot and stir to combine. Nestle the sausages into the sauerkraut mixture. Lock on the lid, select the **PRESSURE COOK** function, and adjust to **HIGH** pressure for 6 minutes. Make sure the steam valve is in the "Sealing" position.

3 When the cooking time is up, let the pressure come down naturally for 10 minutes and then quick-release any remaining pressure. Serve hot, with mustard on the side, if desired.

Tasty Tip: Be sure to purchase smoked (not raw) sausages; they will hold up better under pressure.

BARBECUE MEATLOAF

· · · · · · · · · · · · · ·

Serves 4 to 6

ACTIVE TIME	FUNCTION	TOTAL TIME	RELEASE
10 minutes	Pressure	55 minutes	Quick

This easy meatloaf makes enough to feed four, plus a few extra slices for a cold meatloaf sandwich the next day. For a heartier meal, you can make a side dish of garlic mashed potatoes in the pot at the same time—see the Tasty Tip below.

1½ **pounds ground meatloaf mix (beef and pork)**

1 **cup thick barbecue sauce**

6 **tablespoons dry Italian breadcrumbs**

1 **large carrot, grated**

¼ **cup finely chopped shallots**

1 **large egg, beaten**

Salt and freshly ground black pepper

Tasty Tip: For garlic mashed potatoes, add 4 peeled and halved Yukon Gold potatoes and 4 garlic cloves to the bottom of the pot. Place a tall trivet over the potatoes and put the meatloaf on top. At the end of cooking, drain and mash the potatoes and garlic with a little milk and butter; season to taste.

1 In a large bowl, combine the meat, ¼ cup of the barbecue sauce, the breadcrumbs, carrot, shallots, egg, and ½ teaspoon each salt and pepper. Place a 14-inch-long piece of foil on a work surface. Put another 14-inch piece of foil on top of the first to create a cross. Place the meatloaf mixture in the center of the sheets of foil and form it into a loaf that is about 7 inches in length. Use the side of your hand to create a ½-inch-deep trench in the center of the loaf (this will help the meat cook evenly and hold more of the barbecue sauce). Bring the edges of the foil up, folding them into a little pan with 3- to 4-inch-high sides.

2 Pour 1½ cups of water into the pot. Place the meatloaf in its foil pan on a trivet with handles. Pour the remaining barbecue sauce over the top of the meatloaf, and carefully lower it into the pot on the trivet. Lock on the lid, select the **PRESSURE COOK** function, and adjust to **HIGH** pressure for 25 minutes. Make sure the steam valve is in the "Sealing" position.

3 When the cooking time is up, quick-release the pressure. Carefully lift the meatloaf from the pot (two sets of tongs work well). Drain the drippings from the foil pan and discard. Cut the meatloaf into thick slices and serve.

NORDIC MEATBALLS WITH CREAMY PAN SAUCE

· · · · · · · · · ·

Serves 4

ACTIVE TIME	FUNCTION	TOTAL TIME	RELEASE
22 minutes	Sauté, Pressure	40 minutes	Natural + quick

Rye bread and fresh dill make these meatballs tender and tasty. Add a pinch of allspice
if you have it on hand. Broiling the meatballs builds flavor and is quicker than browning
them in batches in the Instant Pot. Serve over mashed potatoes or boiled egg noodles.

1   slice dark rye sandwich bread, torn into pieces, crusts discarded

¼   cup plus 2 tablespoons cream cheese (3 ounces), at room temperature

1½   cups store-bought beef broth, or homemade (page 228)

1½   pounds meatloaf mix (or ¾ pound *each* ground pork and lean ground beef)

¼   cup chopped fresh dill, or 2½ teaspoons dried dill

    Salt and freshly ground black pepper

1   tablespoon olive oil

½   medium yellow onion, finely chopped

¼   cup all-purpose flour

OPTIONAL GARNISH

    Lingonberry jam or cranberry sauce

1   Preheat the broiler and adjust an oven rack so it is 4 inches from the broiling element. Line a baking sheet with foil and spray with cooking spray.

2   In a large bowl, combine the bread, 2 tablespoons of the cream cheese, and 2 tablespoons of the broth and mix well until the bread is softened to mush. Add the meat, dill, 1 teaspoon salt, and several grinds of pepper. Mix until well combined. Roll into 28 meatballs (about 1½ tablespoons each) and place them on the prepared baking sheet. Broil until browned on one side, about 5 minutes.

3   Meanwhile, put the oil in the pot, select **SAUTÉ**, and adjust to **NORMAL/MEDIUM**. When the oil is hot, add the onion, and cook, stirring frequently, until well browned, 6 minutes. Press **CANCEL**.

4   Transfer the meatballs to the pot, discarding any drippings on the baking sheet. Add the remaining broth to the pot. Lock on the lid, select the **PRESSURE COOK** function, and adjust to **HIGH** pressure for 5 minutes. Make sure the steam valve is in the "Sealing" position.

5 When the cooking time is up, let the pressure come down naturally for 10 minutes and then quick-release the remaining pressure. Use a slotted spoon to transfer the meatballs to a serving dish. Cover with foil.

6 Place the flour in a small bowl and slowly whisk in ¼ cup water until smooth. Select **SAUTÉ** and adjust to **NORMAL/ MEDIUM** heat. Add the flour mixture and remaining cream cheese to the pot. Simmer, whisking constantly, until the sauce is smooth and bubbly, 2 minutes. Press **CANCEL**. Season with salt and pepper. Pour the sauce over the meatballs and serve with lingonberry jam or cranberry sauce, if desired.

Tasty Tip: This recipe produces a blond gravy. Add a teaspoon or two of soy sauce to season the sauce and make it a shade darker, if you like.

RICH PORK RAGU WITH GNOCCHI

· · · · · · · · ·

Serves 8

ACTIVE TIME	FUNCTION	TOTAL TIME	RELEASE
25 minutes	Sauté, Pressure	1 hour 15 minutes	Natural + quick

Also called "Sunday gravy," this Neapolitan specialty is traditionally made by taking a big hunk of pork and simmering it with tomatoes in a pot on the back of the stove for hours. In this streamlined recipe, boneless country-style ribs (strips of shoulder meat) lend rich flavor and cook under high pressure in 20 minutes. This recipe makes enough sauce for four plus enough to freeze for another meal; the sauce improves with time.

3 **pounds boneless country-style pork ribs**

Salt and freshly ground black pepper

2 tablespoons olive oil

1 **medium yellow onion, chopped**

4 **medium garlic cloves, chopped**

2 **teaspoons Italian seasoning**

¼ cup store-bought chicken broth, or homemade (page 227), or water

1 **(28-ounce) can San Marzano-style tomatoes, chopped, with juices**

1 **(17.6-ounce) package fresh gnocchi**

1 Select **SAUTÉ** and adjust to **MORE/HIGH** heat. When the pot is hot, season the pork all over with salt and pepper and drizzle with 1 tablespoon of the oil. Working in two batches, sear the pork until browned on two sides, 5 minutes each batch. Transfer to a plate.

2 Pour the remaining 1 tablespoon oil into the pot. Add the onion and cook until tender, 4 minutes. Add the garlic and 1½ teaspoons of the Italian seasoning and cook until fragrant, 45 seconds. Add the broth or water and scrape up the browned bits on the bottom of the pot. Press **CANCEL**.

3 Return the pork and any accumulated juices to the pot and add the tomatoes. Lock on the lid, select the **PRESSURE COOK** function, and adjust to **MORE/HIGH** pressure for 20 minutes. Make sure the steam valve is in the "Sealing" position. (Or you can **SLOW COOK** it—see page 170.)

4 Meanwhile, cook the gnocchi according to the package instructions.

(recipe continues)

(continued from page 169)

5 When cooking time is up, let the pressure come down naturally for 10 minutes and then quick-release the remaining pressure. Transfer the meat to a cutting board and shred or chop it, discarding any large bits of fat. While you're shredding the meat, select **SAUTÉ**, adjust to **MORE/HIGH** heat, and bring the sauce to a simmer.

6 Liquid fat will pool around the edges of the pot while it's simmering; use a ladle to skim this off and discard. Add the remaining ½ teaspoon Italian seasoning and the shredded meat to the pot and simmer for 1 minute. Season with salt and pepper. Press **CANCEL**. Serve half the sauce with the gnocchi. *(The remaining sauce without the gnocchi can be stored in an airtight container in the refrigerator for up to 5 days or in the freezer for up to 3 months. Reheat gently before serving.)*

Slow Cook It: Increase the broth to 1 cup and the Italian seasoning to 1 tablespoon. In Step 3, select **SLOW COOK**, adjust to **NORMAL/MEDIUM** heat, and set for 10 to 11 hours. Lock on the lid set to "Venting," or use a pan lid that fits snugly on the pot (see Helpful Equipment, page 18). Proceed with the recipe as directed. In Step 6, you may need to increase the simmering time to 20 minutes.

CAROLINA PULLED PORK BARBECUE

· · · · · · · · · · · · ·

Serves 4 to 6

ACTIVE TIME	FUNCTION	TOTAL TIME	RELEASE
10 minutes	Pressure OR Slow, Sauté	1½ hours	Natural + quick

This recipe gives you fork-tender pulled pork barbecue with just 10 minutes of effort. It gets a slightly smoky flavor from smoked paprika. You can substitute ¼ teaspoon liquid smoke for the smoked paprika, if you like. Serve the pork alongside the Smoky Collard Greens on page 218, or put it on hamburger buns and top with coleslaw.

1 (4-pound) boneless pork shoulder or pork butt roast

3 tablespoons packed brown sugar

1 tablespoon seasoning salt (such as Johnny's Fine Foods)

1½ teaspoons smoked paprika

1 cup ketchup

½ cup cider vinegar

1 Trim any excess fat off the outside of the pork and cut the meat into four large pieces. In a small bowl, combine the brown sugar, seasoning salt, and paprika. Rub evenly all over the meat.

2 Combine the ketchup, vinegar, and ½ cup water in the pot. Add the meat and turn to coat in the sauce. Lock on the lid, select the **PRESSURE COOK** function, and adjust to **HIGH** pressure for 40 minutes. Make sure the steam valve is in the "Sealing" position. (Or you can **SLOW COOK** it—see page 172.)

3 When the cooking time is up, let the pressure come down naturally for 15 minutes and then quick-release the remaining pressure.

4 Transfer the pork to a cutting board and shred with two forks, discarding any large chunks of fat. Place in a serving bowl and cover with foil.

(recipe continues)

(continued from page 171)

Tasty Tip: If you prefer spicy barbecue, add ½ to 1 teaspoon red pepper flakes to the pot along with the ketchup.

5   While you're shredding the meat, select **SAUTÉ**, adjust to **MORE/HIGH**, and bring the sauce to a simmer. Skim the liquid fat off the top of the sauce (there may be as much as ½ to ¾ cup) and discard. Press **CANCEL**. Ladle some of the sauce over the pork and serve with the remaining sauce on the side.

Slow Cook It: Double the amounts of ketchup and vinegar. In Step 2, increase the water to 1 cup. Select **SLOW COOK**, adjust to **NORMAL/MEDIUM** heat, and set for 10 to 11 hours. Lock on the lid set to "Venting," or use a pan lid that fits snugly on the pot (see Helpful Equipment, page 18). Proceed with Step 4.

PHILLY CHEESE STEAKS

· · · · · · · · · ·

Serves 4

ACTIVE TIME	FUNCTION	TOTAL TIME	RELEASE
12 minutes	Sauté, Pressure	30 minutes	Natural + quick

Instead of using the traditional (and pricey) rib-eye steaks, I opt for sirloin, flank, or flat iron steaks, browned and cut into thin strips, for this take on the classic sandwich. The sliced meat becomes perfectly tender in just minutes in the Instant Pot. All you have to do then is toast some hoagie buns and roll up your sleeves.

1½ pounds flat iron steak, top sirloin steak, or flank steak, cut to fit into the pot

1 tablespoon olive oil

4 teaspoons steak seasoning or garlic seasoning blend

1 cup store-bought beef broth, or homemade (page 228)

1 large red bell pepper, cut into 1-inch-wide strips

2 tablespoons soy sauce

4 crusty hoagie or sub sandwich rolls, split lengthwise

4 slices provolone or American cheese

1 Select **SAUTÉ** and adjust to **MORE/HIGH** heat. Brush the steak(s) with the oil and rub the steak seasoning into the meat. When the pot is hot, add the steaks in batches and cook until well browned, about 4 minutes per side. Press **CANCEL**.

2 Transfer the steaks to a cutting board and slice against the grain into ¼- to ½-inch-thick slices. Return the meat and accumulated juices on the cutting board to the pot. Add the broth, bell peppers, and soy sauce. Lock on the lid, select the **PRESSURE COOK** function, and adjust to **HIGH** pressure for 5 minutes. Make sure the steam valve is in the "Sealing" position.

3 When the cooking time is up, let the pressure come down naturally for 10 minutes, then quick-release any remaining pressure.

4 Toast the rolls, if desired. With a slotted spoon, remove the beef and vegetables from the pot; reserve the cooking liquid for another use. Mound the beef and peppers on the rolls. Top with slices of cheese and serve.

ONE POT

HERBY PORK CHOPS WITH BUTTERNUT SQUASH

· · · · · · · · · ·
Serves 4

ACTIVE TIME	FUNCTION	TOTAL TIME	RELEASE
20 minutes	Sauté, Pressure	1 hour 5 minutes	Natural + quick

This one-pot meal combines pork in a savory white wine sauce and butternut squash steamed in a basket above the chops. Look for convenient packages of mixed fresh "poultry herbs" (usually rosemary, thyme, and sage) in the produce department. If you can't find it, choose your favorite of the three, or supplement with more if you happen to have them on hand.

3 tablespoons olive oil

4 (6- to 8-ounce) center-cut bone-in pork rib chops, 1 inch thick

Salt and freshly ground black pepper

3 medium garlic cloves, chopped

1 tablespoon plus 1½ teaspoons finely chopped mixed fresh poultry herbs (or your choice of rosemary, thyme, or sage)

½ cup dry white wine

½ cup store-bought chicken broth, or homemade (page 227)

1 medium (2-pound) butternut squash, peeled, seeded, and cut into 1-inch cubes

1 tablespoon cornstarch

1 Put 2 tablespoons of the oil in the pot, select **SAUTÉ**, and adjust to **MORE/HIGH** heat. Season the chops all over with salt and pepper. When the oil is hot, add two of the chops and cook until browned on one side, about 3 minutes. Transfer to a plate and repeat with the remaining chops.

2 Add the garlic and 1 tablespoon of the herbs and cook, stirring constantly, until fragrant, 30 seconds. Add the wine and simmer, scraping up the browned bits from the bottom of the pot, for 2 minutes. Press **CANCEL**. Return the chops and any accumulated juices to the pot and add the broth.

3 Set a steamer basket over the chops. In a large bowl, combine the squash, the remaining 1 tablespoon oil, and the remaining 1½ teaspoons herbs. Season liberally with salt and pepper and place in the steamer basket. Lock on the lid, select the **PRESSURE COOK** function, and adjust to **HIGH** pressure for 10 minutes. Make sure the steam valve is in the "Sealing" position.

(recipe continues)

(continued from page 175)

4   When the cooking time is up, let the pressure come down naturally for 15 minutes and then quick-release the remaining pressure. Transfer the squash to a serving bowl. Transfer the chops to a serving plate.

5   Remove ½ cup of the cooking liquid from the pot and discard. Select **SAUTÉ** and adjust to **MORE/HIGH** heat. When the liquid comes to a simmer, use a ladle to skim off most of the liquid fat that pools around the edges of the pot. In a small bowl, mix the cornstarch with 1 tablespoon cold water. Add the cornstarch mixture to the pot, stir, and simmer until thickened, 1 minute. Press **CANCEL**.

6   Spoon the sauce over the chops and serve with the squash.

ONE POT PORK CHOPS WITH TUSCAN BEANS

· · · · · · · · · ·
Serves 4

ACTIVE TIME	FUNCTION	TOTAL TIME	RELEASE
20 minutes	Sauté, Pressure	50 minutes, plus soaking time	Natural + quick

Bone-in pork chops and soaked cannellini beans cook in the same amount of time in this comforting Tuscan-inspired dish. Serve with rustic bread for scooping up the delicious sauce.

1 **cup dried cannellini beans, picked over and rinsed**

   Salt and freshly ground black pepper

4 **(8-ounce) center-cut bone-in pork chops (¾ to 1 inch thick)**

2 tablespoons olive oil

1 **medium yellow onion, chopped**

¾ cup store-bought chicken broth, or homemade (page 227)

¼ **cup oil-packed sun-dried tomatoes, drained and chopped**

1 **teaspoon dried sage**

   Finely grated zest and juice of ½ lemon

1 Place the beans in a large bowl, cover with cold water and 1 teaspoon salt, and soak at room temperature for 8 to 9 hours. Alternatively, quick-soak the beans: Combine them with several cups of water and 1 teaspoon salt, and boil them on the stove for 1 minute. Let them soak off the heat for 1 hour. Drain.

2 Select **SAUTÉ** and adjust to **MORE/HIGH** heat. Drizzle the chops with 1 tablespoon of the oil and season all over with salt and pepper. When the pot is hot, brown the chops in batches, about 4 minutes for the first batch, 2 minutes for the second batch. Transfer to a plate. (Adjust to **NORMAL/MEDIUM** heat if the pot gets too hot.)

3 Add the remaining 1 tablespoon oil to the pot. Add the onion and sauté, scraping up the browned bits on the bottom of the pot, until tender, 4 minutes. Press **CANCEL**. Add the drained beans, broth, sun-dried tomatoes, sage, and ½ teaspoon salt and stir to combine. Place the pork chops on top of the bean mixture. Lock on the lid, select the **PRESSURE COOK** function, and adjust to **HIGH** pressure for 5 minutes. Make sure the steam valve is in the "Sealing" position.

4 When the cooking time is up, let the pressure come down naturally for 15 minutes and then quick-release any remaining pressure. Stir in the lemon zest and juice. Using a slotted spoon, transfer the chops and beans to plates. Drizzle some of the cooking liquid over the top (you may not need all of it).

Tasty Tip: Buy beans from a store that has a fair amount of food turnover. If the dried beans have been on the shelf (or in the bulk bin) for a long time, they may need a longer cooking time. In the unlikely event that the beans are not done at the end of the cooking time given above, remove the chops from the pot and cover them with foil. Lock on the lid, select **PRESSURE COOK**, and adjust to **HIGH** pressure for an additional 1 to 5 minutes, depending on how hard the beans are.

ROOT BEER–BRAISED SHORT RIBS

··········

Serves 4

ACTIVE TIME	FUNCTION	TOTAL TIME	RELEASE
45 minutes	Sauté, Pressure	1 hour 55 minutes	Natural + quick

You won't be able to identify the soda in this recipe—the flavor melds with the beef, garlic, and vinegar to create a rich, dark sauce that's much more than the sum of its parts. That said, you'll get the best results with an "artisan" root beer or sarsaparilla; they have more depth of flavor and tend to be less sweet than the big brands that cater to kids.

3½ to 4 **pounds meaty English-cut short ribs, fat trimmed**

Salt and freshly ground black pepper

2 tablespoons olive oil

1 **medium onion, sliced through the root end**

4 **medium garlic cloves, thinly sliced**

3 **tablespoons tomato paste**

1 **(12-ounce) bottle good-quality root beer**

½ cup store-bought beef broth, or homemade (page 228)

2 tablespoons cider vinegar

1 Select **SAUTÉ** and adjust to **MORE/HIGH** heat. Season the short ribs all over with salt and several grinds of pepper. Drizzle the meaty sides of the ribs with 1 tablespoon of the oil. When the pot is hot, brown the short ribs in batches, meaty-side down, until well browned, about 5 minutes per batch. Transfer the browned short ribs to a plate. Press **CANCEL**. Pour off the drippings in the pan and return the pot to the appliance.

2 Select **SAUTÉ** and adjust to **NORMAL/MEDIUM** heat. Add the remaining 1 tablespoon oil and the onion to the pot and cook until tender, 4 minutes. Add the garlic and tomato paste and cook until fragrant, 30 seconds. Add the root beer and bring to a simmer, scraping up the browned bits on the bottom of the pot. Add the broth and vinegar and stir to combine. Return the short ribs and accumulated juices to the pot, standing the ribs on their skinny sides so they are partially submerged in the cooking liquid. Lock on the lid, select the **PRESSURE COOK** function, and adjust to **HIGH** pressure for 40 minutes. Make sure the steam valve is in the "Sealing" position. (Or you can **SLOW COOK** it—see opposite.)

3 When the cooking time is up, let the pressure come down naturally for 15 minutes and then quick-release the remaining pressure. Carefully transfer the ribs to a large serving bowl and cover with foil. A few may fall off their bones; just discard the bones and know that the meat is going to be very tender.

4 Select **SAUTÉ** and adjust to **HIGH/MORE**. Liquid fat will pool around the edges of the pot while it's simmering; use a ladle to skim off the fat and discard it (see Tasty Tip, below). You may get as much as 1 to 1½ cups fat; short ribs are a fatty cut of beef. Simmer the sauce until reduced by half, about 10 minutes. Pour the sauce over the ribs and serve.

Tasty Tip: If you have a fat separator (see Helpful Equipment, page 18), use it to defat the sauce in Step 3 to save time instead of skimming. Return the defatted liquid to the pot and simmer as directed.

Slow Cook It: In Step 2, select the **SLOW COOK** function, adjust to **NORMAL/MEDIUM** heat, and set for 10 to 11 hours. Lock on the lid set to "Venting," or use a pan lid that fits snugly on the pot (see Helpful Equipment, page 18).

KOREAN SHORT RIB BIBIMBAP BOWLS

. . . .
Serves 4

ACTIVE TIME	FUNCTION	TOTAL TIME	RELEASE
10 minutes	Pressure	35 minutes, plus marinating time	Natural + quick

Flanken-style ribs are cut across the ribs into ½-inch-thick slices with small bones between them. Find them at the meat counter of your grocery store or at Asian markets; do not use meaty thick-cut English-style short ribs for this recipe. Marinate the ribs in Korean kalbi marinade (available at most grocery stores and Asian markets) for as long as you can for the best flavor.

3 pounds flanken-style short ribs

1 (9- to 12-ounce) bottle Korean kalbi marinade sauce (such as CJ Korean BBQ Kalbi Marinade)

1½ cups short-grain white rice, rinsed well and drained in a sieve

4 large eggs

1 cup napa cabbage kimchi

OPTIONAL GARNISH

Gochujang (Korean red chile paste)

1 Place the short ribs in a large nonreactive bowl or a large zip-top bag and add the marinade. Cover or seal and refrigerate for at least 1 hour and up to 24 hours.

2 Place the ribs and the marinade in the Instant Pot, arranging the ribs on their edges and curving them into the pot so they all fit. Place a tall trivet over the ribs. In a 7-inch round metal baking pan, combine the rice with 1½ cups cold water. Cover the pan tightly with foil. Place the baking pan on the tall trivet above the ribs. Lock on the lid, select the **PRESSURE COOK** function, and adjust to **HIGH** pressure for 10 minutes. Make sure the steam valve is in the "Sealing" position. (Or you can **SLOW COOK** it—see page 184.)

3 When the cooking time is up, let the pressure come down naturally for 10 minutes and then quick-release the remaining pressure.

(recipe continues)

(continued from page 183)

4 Lift the rice in the baking pan out of the pot, fluff with a fork, and set aside. Transfer the ribs to a large plate or cutting board, cut into manageable pieces with clean kitchen scissors, and spoon a few tablespoons of the cooking liquid over them. Cover with foil.

5 Spray a large nonstick skillet with cooking spray and place over medium-high heat. Break the eggs into the pan and cook until the whites are set, about 3 minutes.

6 Divide the rice among four bowls. Top the rice with the ribs, eggs, and kimchi. Serve with gochujang, if desired.

Slow Cook It: Skip the marinating time in Step 1. In Step 2, cook the rice separately. For the ribs, select **SLOW COOK**, adjust to **NORMAL/MEDIUM** heat, and set for 8 to 9 hours. Lock on the lid set to "Venting," or use a pan lid that fits snugly on the pot (see Helpful Equipment, page 18). Proceed with the recipe as directed.

ONE POT

FIG-GLAZED HAM WITH DILL POTATOES

· · · · · · · · · · · · ·

Serves 4 to 6

ACTIVE TIME	FUNCTION	TOTAL TIME	RELEASE
15 minutes	Pressure OR Slow, Sauté	1½ hours	Natural

Cooking ham in the Instant Pot produces juicy meat infused with a zesty fig-and-mustard glaze in this recipe. Fig jam is available in the cheese department of some grocery stores and online. If you can't find fig jam, use thick-cut orange marmalade instead. Don't be tempted to use a larger ham: A 3-pound boneless ham is as large as you want to go in a 6-quart Instant Pot. Spiral-sliced hams tend to dry out when cooked under pressure, so opt for a boneless, unsliced ham.

1	**(3-pound) smoked boneless ham (not spiral-sliced)**
½	**cup fig jam or orange marmalade**
½	**cup grainy mustard**
½	**cup packed brown sugar**
1½ to 2	**pounds small Yukon Gold potatoes (2 to 3 inches in diameter)**
2	**tablespoons chopped fresh dill**
2 to 3	**tablespoons olive oil**
	Salt and freshly ground black pepper

1 Place ½ cup of water in the pot. Set a trivet with handles in the pot and place the ham cut-side down on the trivet. In a small bowl, mix the jam, mustard, and brown sugar until smooth. Spread over the ham (it's fine if it drips into the water below). Place the potatoes on top of and around the sides of the ham. Lock on the lid, select the **PRESSURE COOK** function, and adjust to **LOW** pressure for 45 minutes. Make sure the steam valve is in the "Sealing" position. (Or you can **SLOW COOK** it—see page 186.)

2 When the cooking time is up, let the pressure come down naturally. An instant-read thermometer should read 140°F. If not, reseal the lid and cook under **LOW** pressure for an additional 5 minutes.

3 Transfer the potatoes to a serving bowl and toss with the dill, olive oil, and salt and pepper. Cover with foil and set aside. Transfer the ham to a cutting board or serving platter and tent with foil.

(recipe continues)

(continued from page 185)

4 Select **SAUTÉ** and adjust to **MORE/HIGH** heat. Simmer the cooking liquid until it is reduced by about half, 10 minutes. Press **CANCEL**. Slice the ham, drizzle with some of the cooking liquid, and serve with the potatoes.

Tasty Tip: If you like the traditional flavor of cloves with ham, add 6 whole cloves to the liquid in the bottom of the pot. They will infuse the steam and glaze with clove flavor.

Slow Cook It: If using the SLOW COOK function, in Step 1 omit the trivet and increase the water to 1 cup. Select **SLOW COOK,** adjust to **NORMAL/MEDIUM** heat, and set for 7 to 8 hours. Lock on the lid set to "Venting," or use a pan lid that fits snugly on the pot (see Helpful Equipment, page 18). Proceed with the recipe as directed, simmering the cooking liquid in Step 4 for 15 to 20 minutes.

HONEY BARBECUE SPARERIBS

· · · · · · · · · ·

Serves 4

ACTIVE TIME	FUNCTION	TOTAL TIME	RELEASE
10 minutes	Pressure	1 hour	Natural + quick

These ribs are cooked in homemade sweet-spicy barbecue sauce in the Instant Pot until fall-apart tender. Broiling them briefly will give them an addictive glazed, lightly charred exterior. Serve with Smoky Collard Greens (page 218) or German Potato Salad (page 205).

2 racks baby back ribs (3 pounds; about 4 ribs each), cut into 5- to 6-inch portions

2 tablespoons chili powder

1 cup ketchup

½ cup store-bought chicken broth, or homemade (page 227)

⅓ cup honey

3 tablespoons grainy mustard

2 tablespoons toasted sesame oil

1 tablespoon red wine vinegar

1 Rub the ribs all over with the chili powder. In the pot, combine the ketchup, broth, honey, mustard, sesame oil, and vinegar and whisk until the honey has dissolved. Dunk the ribs in the sauce to coat them and then arrange them standing upright against the sides of the pot. Lock on the lid, select the **PRESSURE COOK** function, and adjust to **HIGH** pressure for 25 minutes. Make sure the steam valve is in the "Sealing" position.

2 Preheat the broiler and adjust an oven rack so that it is 4 inches below the broiler element. Line a baking sheet with foil. When the cooking time is up, let the pressure come down naturally for 15 minutes and then quick-release the remaining pressure. Transfer the ribs with tongs to the prepared baking sheet meat-side up; they will be very tender, so be gentle when transferring them out of the pot. Stir the cooking liquid and spoon a generous amount over the ribs. Broil the ribs until browned in places, 5 minutes.

Tasty Tip: The remaining cooking liquid/barbecue sauce can be saved for another use. Select SAUTÉ, adjust to NORMAL/MEDIUM heat, and simmer the sauce until thickened, 5 minutes. Using a ladle, skim off the liquid fat that floats to the top and discard. Press CANCEL. Store in the refrigerator for up to 1 week. Use as a basting sauce for chicken, pork, or beef.

PORK VINDALOO

· · · · · · · · · ·

Serves 4

ACTIVE TIME	FUNCTION	TOTAL TIME	RELEASE
10 minutes	Sauté, Pressure OR Slow	50 minutes	Quick

In this streamlined spin on the classic Indian dish, cubed pork shoulder is simmered with garam masala—an Indian blend that always contains the five C's: cardamom, coriander, cumin, cinnamon, and cloves. Look for garam masala at well-stocked grocery stores and online; curry powder will do in a pinch. The combination of red wine vinegar and tomatoes with green chilies makes this dish mildly piquant; if you'd like it authentically spicy, add a chopped serrano chile.

1 tablespoon canola oil

1 medium yellow onion, halved and sliced through the root end

2 pounds boneless pork shoulder, cut into 2-inch cubes

4 teaspoons garam masala spice blend or curry powder

¼ cup store-bought chicken broth, or homemade (page 227), or water

1 (10-ounce) can Ro-Tel tomatoes with green chilies, with juice, or 1¼ cups canned diced tomatoes with green chilies

1 Put the oil in the pot, select **SAUTÉ**, and adjust to **NORMAL/MEDIUM** heat. Add the onion and a small handful (6 or 7 pieces) of pork and cook, stirring frequently, until there are some browned bits on the bottom of the pot, 5 minutes. Press **CANCEL**. Add the garam masala and stir to combine. Add the broth and scrape up the browned bits on the bottom of the pot.

2 Add the tomatoes and vinegar to the pot. Season the remaining pork all over with salt and pepper. Add the pork to the pot and stir to coat it with the sauce. Lock on the lid, select the **PRESSURE COOK** function, and adjust to **HIGH** pressure for 30 minutes. Make sure the steam valve is in the "Sealing" position. (Alternatively, you can **SLOW COOK** it—see opposite.)

2 tablespoons red wine vinegar

Salt and freshly ground
black pepper

1 **tablespoon cornstarch**

¼ **cup chopped fresh cilantro**

OPTIONAL

1 serrano chile, chopped

3 When the cooking time is up, quick-release the pressure. In a small bowl, combine the cornstarch with 1½ tablespoons water. Select **SAUTÉ** and adjust to **NORMAL/MEDIUM** heat. Add the cornstarch mixture to the pot, stir gently (try not to break up the pork too much), and simmer until bubbly, 1 minute. Fold in the cilantro and season with salt and pepper. Stir in the serrano, if desired, and serve.

Tasty Tip: Substitute boneless, skinless chicken thighs for the pork. Reduce the pressure-cooking time to 10 minutes.

Slow Cook It: Increase the broth to 1 cup, the garam masala to 5 teaspoons, and the vinegar to 3 tablespoons. In Step 2, select **SLOW COOK**, adjust to **NORMAL/MEDIUM** heat, and set for 7 to 8 hours. Lock on the lid set to "Venting," or use a pan lid that fits snugly on the pot (see Helpful Equipment, page 18). In Step 3, increase the cornstarch to 1½ tablespoons.

CHINESE BRAISED PORK AND EGGPLANT

··········
Serves 4

ACTIVE TIME	FUNCTION	TOTAL TIME	RELEASE
10 minutes	Sauté, Pressure	30 minutes	Quick

Hand-chopping the pork in this recipe adds an interesting springy texture to this dish; partially freezing the meat will make the job much easier. Long, slender Japanese eggplant is less bitter than standard European globe eggplant and doesn't need to be salted to draw out its bitterness, so it's worth seeking out. Serve this braise by itself or on top of hot steamed rice or yakisoba noodles.

1 **medium (1-pound) Japanese eggplant, cut crosswise into 1½-inch-thick slices, or globe eggplant cut into 2-inch chunks**

Salt and freshly ground black pepper

¼ cup canned chicken broth, or homemade (page 227)

3 **tablespoons soy sauce**

1 tablespoon balsamic or red wine vinegar

1 **tablespoon sambal oelek (chili garlic paste)**

1½ **pounds thin-cut boneless pork chops, frozen for 15 minutes**

1 tablespoon canola oil

1 If using globe eggplant, toss the cubes with ¾ teaspoon salt and set aside in a colander for 20 minutes to draw out the bitter juices. Pat the eggplant dry with paper towels. (Skip this step if you're using Japanese eggplant.)

2 In a medium bowl, combine the broth, soy sauce, vinegar, and sambal oelek; set aside. Trim the fat from the chops and discard. Chop the pork into roughly ½-inch pieces. Season with salt and pepper.

3 Put the oil in the pot, select **SAUTÉ**, and adjust to **MORE/HIGH** heat. When the oil is hot, add the pork and ginger and cook, stirring frequently, until the pork is opaque and white all over, 3 minutes. Press **CANCEL**.

4 Add the broth mixture and stir. Add the eggplant to the pot, but do not stir it into the sauce. Select the **PRESSURE COOK** function and adjust to **HIGH** pressure for 3 minutes. Make sure the steam valve is in the "Sealing" position.

1 tablespoon finely chopped
  fresh ginger

1 tablespoon cornstarch

OPTIONAL GARNISH

1 cup chopped dry-roasted
  peanuts

5 When the cooking time is up, quick-release the pressure. Using a slotted spoon, gently transfer the eggplant and most of the pork to a large serving bowl; set aside. In a small bowl, mix the cornstarch and 1 tablespoon cold water. Add the cornstarch mixture to the pot, select **SAUTÉ,** and adjust to **MORE/HIGH** heat. Simmer until thickened and bubbly, 1 minute. Press **CANCEL**. Pour the sauce over the pork and eggplant, stir gently to combine, and serve immediately, garnished with peanuts, if desired.

LAMB GYROS

··········
Serves 4

ACTIVE TIME	FUNCTION	TOTAL TIME	RELEASE
20 minutes	Pressure	40 minutes, plus marinating time	Natural + quick

Thinly sliced lamb becomes melt-in-your-mouth tender in just 10 minutes under high pressure. Allow at least a few hours of marinating time to infuse the meat with garlic and oregano—it's key to making these sandwiches taste authentic.

2 **pounds boneless leg of lamb**

2 tablespoons olive oil

4 **medium garlic cloves, finely chopped**

2 **teaspoons dried oregano**

Salt and freshly ground black pepper

1 cup store-bought beef broth, or homemade (page 228)

4 **pita breads or flatbreads**

1 **cup plain full-fat Greek yogurt**

½ **cup seeded and finely chopped cucumber**

OPTIONAL GARNISHES

Chopped tomatoes

Chopped romaine lettuce

Thinly sliced red onions

1 With a boning knife, trim the fat and any silvery connective tissue from the meat. Slice the meat into ⅛- to ¼-inch-thick slices. Cut the slices into strips about 1½ inches wide. In a nonreactive bowl or zip-top bag, combine the lamb strips, oil, 1 tablespoon of the garlic, the oregano, ¾ teaspoon salt, and several grinds of pepper. Cover or seal and refrigerate for at least 2 hours or up to 24 hours.

2 Place the meat and any marinade clinging to it in the pot. Add the broth and stir to combine. Lock on the lid, select the **PRESSURE COOK** function, and adjust to **HIGH** pressure for 10 minutes. Make sure the steam valve is in the "Sealing" position.

3 When the cooking time is up, let the pressure come down naturally for 10 minutes and then quick-release the remaining pressure.

4 Toast the pita breads or flatbreads in a toaster or toaster oven until warm and pliable. In a small bowl, combine the yogurt, cucumber, and remaining garlic. Use tongs to transfer the lamb to the pita breads; leave the cooking liquid in the pot. Top the sandwiches with the yogurt mixture and garnishes, if desired.

Tasty Tip:
If your family are not fans of lamb, use thinly sliced beef top round.

LAMB TAGINE

· · · · · · · · · ·

Serves 4

ACTIVE TIME	FUNCTION	TOTAL TIME	RELEASE
20 minutes	Sauté, Pressure	1 hour 15 minutes	Natural + quick

Sweet and savory, this meltingly tender braised lamb dish is traditionally served on top of couscous in Morocco. The recipe is mild; add fiery harissa (spiced red chile paste) if you'd like it spicier, but keep in mind that a little goes a long way.

2½ **pounds blade lamb steaks, meat cut off the bones into 1½-inch chunks, bones reserved**

2 tablespoons olive oil

Salt and freshly ground black pepper

1 **medium yellow onion, sliced through root end**

4 **teaspoons ras el hanout seasoning (see page 198)**

1½ cups store-bought beef broth, or homemade (page 228)

2 **large carrots, peeled and cut into 1-inch pieces**

¼ **cup dates, pitted and roughly chopped**

¼ **cup oil-packed sun-dried tomatoes, chopped**

1 tablespoon white wine vinegar

1 Select **SAUTÉ** and adjust to **MORE/HIGH** heat. Toss the lamb meat with the oil and season all over with salt and several grinds of pepper. When the pot is hot, add half the meat and cook, stirring occasionally, until browned, 8 minutes.

2 Add the remaining lamb, the onion, and ras el hanout to the pot and cook, stirring occasionally, until the onion softens, 5 minutes. Add the broth, carrots, dates, and sun-dried tomatoes. Place the bones in the pot on top of the other ingredients. Press **CANCEL**.

3 Lock on the lid, select **PRESSURE COOK,** and adjust to **HIGH** pressure for 25 minutes. Make sure the steam valve is in the "Sealing" position. (Or you can **SLOW COOK** it—see opposite.) When the cooking time is up, let the pressure come down naturally for 15 minutes and then quick-release any remaining pressure. Discard the bones.

4 Select **SAUTÉ** and adjust to **MORE/HIGH** heat. Add the vinegar to the pot and stir to combine. When the liquid comes to a simmer, use a ladle to spoon off most of the liquid fat that

OPTIONAL GARNISHES

Cooked couscous

Harissa

pools around the edges of the pot. Press **CANCEL**. Season with salt and pepper. If desired, serve over couscous with dabs of harissa.

Tasty Tip: Substitute precut lamb stew meat for the blade steaks for quicker prep time; you may need to increase the cooking time by a few minutes depending on what cut the stew meat is.

Slow Cook It: In Step 3, select **SLOW COOK** function, adjust to **NORMAL/MEDIUM** heat, and set for 7 to 8 hours. Lock on the lid set to "Venting," or use a pan lid that fits snugly on the pot (see Helpful Equipment, page 18).

MOROCCAN MEATBALLS

Serves 4

ACTIVE TIME	FUNCTION	TOTAL TIME	RELEASE
20 minutes	Pressure	1 hour	Natural + quick

These zesty meatballs contain *ras el hanout*, a Moroccan spice blend (the name means "top of the shop," as in the best spices a shop has to offer). Look for the spice blend and bottles of sweet-tangy pomegranate molasses at well-stocked grocery stores, Middle Eastern shops, and online. The recipe makes lots of sauce with the idea that you'll use some of it to whip up a quick side dish of couscous.

1½ **pounds ground lamb or beef**

1 **cup plus 3 tablespoons store-bought chicken broth, or homemade (page 227)**

½ **cup finely chopped sweet onion**

⅓ **cup dry plain breadcrumbs**

4 **tablespoons pomegranate molasses**

4 **teaspoons ras el hanout Moroccan spice blend**

Salt and freshly ground black pepper

1 **(15-ounce) can fire-roasted diced tomatoes with garlic**

OPTIONAL SIDE DISH

¾ cup instant couscous

1 In a large bowl, combine the lamb, 3 tablespoons of the broth, the onion, breadcrumbs, 1 tablespoon of the pomegranate molasses, the spice blend, ¾ teaspoon salt, and ½ teaspoon pepper. Mix until well combined and then roll into 32 meatballs, about 1 heaping tablespoon each.

2 Combine the 1 cup remaining broth, the tomatoes, and the remaining 3 tablespoons pomegranate molasses in the pot and stir to combine. Add the meatballs (it's fine to stack them in two layers, if necessary). Lock on the lid, select the **PRESSURE COOK** function, and adjust to **HIGH** pressure for 5 minutes. Make sure the steam valve is in the "Sealing" position.

3 When the cooking time is up, let the pressure come down naturally for 10 minutes and then quick-release the remaining pressure. Use a slotted spoon to transfer the meatballs to a serving dish. Using a ladle, skim off the liquid fat that pools around the edges of the pot and discard. Pour the cooking liquid over the meatballs (reserving 1¼ cups for the couscous, if you're using it) and serve.

4   If you'd like to serve the meatballs with couscous, place the couscous in a medium serving bowl. Pour 1½ cups of the defatted cooking liquid over the couscous, cover, and let stand for 5 minutes. Fluff with a fork and serve with the meatballs.

Tasty Tip: If you can't find ras el hanout, substitute garam masala or equal parts ground cumin, coriander, ginger, and paprika.

Tasty Tip: No pomegranate molasses? No problem. Substitute a mix of equal parts honey and balsamic vinegar. It won't have quite the same tang, but it will be delicious!

SIDES

SWEET SRIRACHA-GLAZED ACORN SQUASH

....
Serves 4

ACTIVE TIME	FUNCTION	TOTAL TIME	RELEASE
5 minutes	Pressure	20 minutes	Natural + quick

Sweet and a bit spicy, this updated spin on acorn squash roasted with brown sugar is a good candidate to serve alongside holiday turkey or roast. Add toasted chopped pecans as a garnish if you're feeling fancy.

2 tablespoons butter, at room temperature

2 tablespoons packed brown sugar

1 teaspoon to 1 tablespoon Sriracha hot sauce

1 medium (2-pound) acorn squash, halved and seeded

Salt and freshly ground black pepper

OPTIONAL GARNISH

½ cup chopped toasted pecans

1 Place a trivet or steamer basket in the bottom of the pot and add 1½ cups water. In a small bowl, blend the butter, brown sugar, and the Sriracha. Prick the inside of the squash halves with a fork, sprinkle with salt and pepper, and smear the butter mixture all over the inside of the squash.

2 Carefully place the squash cut-side up on the trivet, making sure that the halves don't tilt; you don't want the butter mixture to spill out of the squash as it melts. Lock on the lid, select the **PRESSURE COOK** function, and adjust to **HIGH** pressure for 5 minutes. Make sure the steam valve is in the "Sealing" position.

3 When the cooking time is up, let the pressure come down naturally for 10 minutes and then quick-release the remaining pressure. Using a spatula and tongs, carefully transfer the squash from the pot to a serving plate, making sure not to spill the liquid in the center. Cut each half into two wedges and serve warm, garnished with the pecans, if desired.

Tasty Tip: This recipe works with small butternut squash and carnival squash, too.

GERMAN POTATO SALAD

· · · · · · · · · ·

Serves 6

ACTIVE TIME	FUNCTION	TOTAL TIME	RELEASE
10 minutes	Sauté, Pressure	30 minutes	Quick

This hearty, warm potato salad is great served with the Bratwurst with Sauerkraut and Cider on page 163 or with Honey Barbecue Spareribs (page 189). The salad can be made ahead, but it's best to gently reheat it in the microwave until just warm before serving.

8 ounces applewood-smoked bacon, chopped

½ cup store-bought chicken broth, or homemade (page 227)

6 tablespoons white wine vinegar

2½ tablespoons grainy mustard

2 tablespoons packed light brown sugar

2 teaspoons caraway seeds

½ teaspoon salt, plus more for seasoning

3 pounds small red potatoes, unpeeled, cut into ¾-inch chunks

½ cup finely chopped sweet onion (such as Walla Walla or Vidalia)

Freshly ground black pepper

1 Put the bacon in the pot, select **SAUTÉ**, and adjust to **NORMAL/MEDIUM** heat. Cook, stirring frequently, until crisp and browned, 8 minutes. Press **CANCEL**. With a slotted spoon, transfer the bacon to a paper towel–lined plate. Reserve 2 tablespoons of the drippings in a small bowl for the dressing and discard the remaining drippings.

2 Place the broth, vinegar, mustard, brown sugar, caraway seeds, and ½ teaspoon salt in the pot and whisk to combine. Place a steamer basket in the pot and add the potatoes to the basket. Lock on the lid, select the **PRESSURE COOK** function, and adjust to **HIGH** pressure for 7 minutes. Make sure the steam valve is in the "Sealing" position.

3 When the cooking time is up, quick-release the pressure. Carefully remove the steamer basket and turn the potatoes into a large bowl. Pour the cooking liquid and the reserved bacon drippings over the potatoes. Add the onion, season with salt and several grinds of pepper, and toss gently with a rubber spatula to combine. Serve warm.

Tasty Tip: Skip the bacon to make this salad vegetarian; substitute good extra-virgin olive oil for the bacon drippings.

CORN ON THE COB, FOUR WAYS

· · · · · · · · · ·
Serves 4

ACTIVE TIME	FUNCTION	TOTAL TIME	RELEASE
5 minutes	Pressure	25 minutes	Quick

The last thing you want to do in the height of summer when corn is in season is get a huge pot of water boiling! With the Instant Pot, you can cook corn on the cob in just a few minutes under pressure without heating up the whole house. Sure, corn on the cob is fine with butter and salt, but why not dress it up with one of these four simple flavor combinations?

FOR THE CORN

    4 ears corn, shucked

FOR MEXICAN CORN ON THE COB

   ⅓ cup mayonnaise

   ¼ cup finely chopped fresh cilantro

   2 teaspoons ground New Mexican chile powder

   ½ cup crumbled aged Cotija or feta cheese

FOR MAPLE-BARBECUE CORN ON THE COB

   4 tablespoons (½ stick) room-temperature butter

   2 tablespoons maple syrup

   4 teaspoons thick barbecue sauce

      Garlic salt

1 Place a trivet with handles or a steamer basket in the pot and pour in 1½ cups warm water. Put the corn in the steamer (cutting the corn cobs in half if necessary to make them fit). Lock on the lid, select the **PRESSURE COOK** function, and adjust to **HIGH** pressure for 2 minutes. Make sure the steam valve is in the "Sealing" position.

2 When the cooking time is up, quick-release the pressure.

3 **For Mexican corn,** spread the mayonnaise on the corn with a rubber spatula and sprinkle with the cilantro, chile powder, and cheese.

For maple-barbecue corn, in a medium bowl, whisk together the butter, maple syrup, and barbecue sauce. Spread the mixture on the corn and sprinkle with garlic salt.

FOR HOT WINGS-STYLE CORN ON THE COB

4   tablespoons (½ stick) butter, at room temperature

2   tablespoons hot sauce

4   teaspoons honey

½   cup crumbled blue cheese

1¼ teaspoons celery salt

FOR FRENCH CORN ON THE COB

½   cup soft herb and garlic cheese spread (such as Boursin), at room temperature

2   tablespoons finely chopped fresh chives

    Freshly ground black pepper

For hot wings–style corn, in a medium bowl, whisk together the butter, hot sauce, and honey. Spread on the corn and then roll the cobs in the blue cheese and sprinkle with the celery salt.

For French corn, spread the cheese spread all over the cobs. Roll in the chives and season with pepper.

INDIAN-SPICED BASMATI RICE

· · · · · · · · · ·

Serves 4

ACTIVE TIME	FUNCTION	TOTAL TIME	RELEASE
5 minutes	Sauté, Pressure	30 minutes	Natural + quick

Sure, this turmeric-hued rice is a great side dish for Indian food, but it also pairs beautifully with grilled fish and meats. I like Lundberg brand California-grown basmati rice because it holds up better in the pressure cooker than delicate imported basmati rice. Look for it at well-stocked supermarkets.

2 tablespoons canola oil

3 medium garlic cloves, finely chopped

1 tablespoon finely chopped fresh ginger

1½ cups California basmati rice (such as Lundberg brand), rinsed and drained

1½ teaspoons garam masala or curry powder

½ teaspoon ground turmeric
Salt

1 cup frozen peas

1 Put the oil in the pot, select **SAUTÉ**, and adjust to **NORMAL/MEDIUM** heat. When the oil is hot, add the garlic and ginger and cook, stirring frequently, until fragrant, 45 seconds. Press **CANCEL**.

2 Add the rice, garam marsala, and turmeric and stir to coat. Add 1½ cups water and ¾ teaspoon salt. Sprinkle the peas over the top of the rice. Lock on the lid, select the **PRESSURE COOK** function, and adjust to **HIGH** pressure for 6 minutes. Make sure the steam valve is in the "Sealing" position.

3 When the cooking time is up, let the pressure come down naturally for 10 minutes and then quick-release the remaining pressure. Fluff with a fork and serve.

Tasty Tip: For a richer flavor, substitute ghee for the oil and add ½ cup chopped roasted cashews before serving.

SPANISH RICE

· · · · · · · · · ·

Serves 4

ACTIVE TIME	FUNCTION	TOTAL TIME	RELEASE
5 minutes	Sauté, Pressure	30 minutes	Natural + quick

Serve this easy side dish with Smoky Shredded Beef Tacos (page 161), grilled meats or seafood, or as a burrito filling along with cooked beans (which you can also cook in the Instant Pot; see page 225). Make sure to use good-quality long-grain rice; cheaper brands tend to have a lot of broken grains that make for mushy rice.

2   tablespoons olive oil

1   **small onion, finely chopped**

1   **cup chopped green bell pepper**

1½ **cups long-grain rice, rinsed and drained**

2   **tablespoons taco seasoning (see Tasty Tip, below)**

⅔   **cup V8 tomato juice (1 small 5.5-ounce can)**

1 Put the oil in the pot, select **SAUTÉ**, and adjust to **NORMAL/ MEDIUM** heat. When the oil is hot, add the onion and bell pepper and cook, stirring frequently, until tender, 4 minutes. Press **CANCEL**. Add the rice and taco seasoning and stir to coat the rice with the vegetables and oil.

2 Add 1¾ cups water and the tomato juice and stir to combine. Lock on the lid, select the **PRESSURE COOK** function, and adjust to **HIGH** pressure for 4 minutes. Make sure the steam valve is in the "Sealing" position.

3 When the cooking time is up, let the pressure come down naturally for 5 minutes and then quick-release the remaining pressure. Fluff with a fork and serve.

Tasty Tip: Be sure to purchase taco seasoning that does not contain cornstarch or other thickeners. I like Simply Organic Southwestern Taco Seasoning.

CREAMY OR CRISPY PARMESAN POLENTA

· · · · · · · · · ·

Serves 4

ACTIVE TIME	FUNCTION	TOTAL TIME	RELEASE
5 minutes	Sauté, Pressure	35 minutes	Natural + quick

Finally, polenta without lumps that doesn't require laborious stirring over the stove! The Instant Pot LOW setting cooks polenta perfectly with no lumps and very little elbow grease on your part. Serve it smooth and creamy as a base for meat dishes or pasta sauce, or chill the polenta until firm and then pan-fry or broil squares for a different spin.

2 tablespoons olive oil

2 **medium garlic cloves, thinly sliced**

4 cups store-bought chicken or vegetable broth, or homemade (page 227 or 226), warmed

1 **bay leaf**

Salt and freshly ground black pepper

1 **cup polenta (not quick-cooking)**

½ **cup grated Parmesan cheese**

1 Place the oil in the pot, select **SAUTÉ**, and adjust to **NORMAL/ MEDIUM** heat. When the oil is hot, add the garlic and cook, stirring frequently, until fragrant, 30 seconds. Add the broth, bay leaf, and ½ teaspoon salt. When the liquid comes to a simmer, gradually whisk in the polenta. Press **CANCEL**.

2 Lock on the lid, select the **PRESSURE COOK** function, and adjust to **LOW** pressure for 9 minutes. Make sure the steam valve is in the "Sealing" position.

3 When the cooking time is up, let the pressure come down naturally for 10 minutes and then quick-release the remaining pressure. Unlock the lid. It will look watery at first, but will come together and thicken as it stands. Whisk in the cheese and season with salt and pepper. Discard the bay leaf before serving.

Tasty Tip:

The cheese is adaptable here—substitute cheddar or blue cheese for the Parmesan, or stir in mascarpone (Italian cream cheese) for extra-creamy polenta.

4 For solid polenta to pan-fry or broil, transfer the polenta to a storage container and refrigerate, uncovered, until solid, at least 2 hours. Cut into squares and pan-fry in a nonstick sauté pan with a few tablespoons of olive oil over medium heat until golden brown, about 5 minutes per side. To broil, spread squares of polenta on a foil-lined baking sheet, drizzle with oil, sprinkle with a little Parmesan cheese, and broil 4 inches from the broiler element until the cheese is bubbly, 6 minutes.

FAUX GRATIN POTATOES

· · · · · · · · · ·

Serves 4

ACTIVE TIME	FUNCTION	TOTAL TIME	RELEASE
15 minutes	Sauté, Pressure	35 minutes	Natural + quick

Cheesy au gratin potatoes take at least an hour in the oven. In this time-saving recipe, the potatoes are cooked in the Instant Pot in just 2 minutes and then broiled for a melty, crusty cheese topping. It's important to be consistent when slicing the potatoes so they cook evenly. To make slicing easier, use a mandoline slicer or the 6mm slicing disk on a food processor. If you're slicing the spuds by hand, cut a thin slice off one side of each potato and rotate them so they sit flat on the cutting board; this will steady them and make slicing safer.

2 tablespoons butter

2 medium garlic cloves, sliced

2 pounds Yukon Gold potatoes, peeled and cut into ¼-inch-thick slices

Salt and freshly ground black pepper

⅔ cup store-bought vegetable or chicken broth, or homemade (page 226 or 227)

1½ cups grated cheese of your choice (cheddar, Gruyère, or Swiss; 6 ounces)

¼ cup heavy cream, warmed

1 Put the butter in the pot, select **SAUTÉ,** and adjust to **NORMAL/MEDIUM** heat. When the butter has melted, add the garlic and cook until fragrant, 45 seconds. Press **CANCEL**.

2 Add the potatoes, 1 teaspoon salt, and several grinds of pepper and stir to coat the potatoes with the garlic butter. Add the broth. Lock on the lid, select the **PRESSURE COOK** function, and adjust to **HIGH** pressure for 2 minutes. Make sure the steam valve is in the "Sealing" position.

3 When the cooking time is up, let the pressure come down naturally for 1 minute and then quick-release the remaining pressure.

4 Preheat a broiler and set an oven rack so it is 6 inches below the broiling element. Pour the potato mixture into an 8-inch square baking dish and gently fold in 1 cup of the cheese and the cream with a rubber spatula. Sprinkle the remaining ½ cup cheese over the top and broil until browned and bubbly, 3 to 5 minutes. Serve immediately.

CREAMY MASHED POTATOES WITH KALE

· · · · · · · · · · · · · ·
Serves 4 to 6

ACTIVE TIME	FUNCTION	TOTAL TIME	RELEASE
10 minutes	Pressure, Sauté	35 minutes	Quick

Called colcannon in Ireland, this clever side dish makes buttery mashed potatoes healthier and tastier by adding kale to the pot. It's a great way to get your kiddos to eat their greens, but you can omit the kale if you'd prefer.

4 **medium russet potatoes (2 pounds), peeled and quartered**

Salt

1 **medium (8-ounce) bunch lacinato kale, tough center rib discarded, leaves chopped**

4 **tablespoons (½ stick) unsalted butter, at room temperature**

4 **green onions, thinly sliced**

¼ to ½ **cup whole milk or heavy cream**

Tasty Tip: Add a few garlic cloves to the water in Step 1 if you like.

1 Place the potatoes in the pot and add 1 cup of water. Sprinkle with ½ teaspoon salt. Put the kale on top of the potatoes, but don't stir it in. Lock on the lid, select the **PRESSURE COOK** function, and adjust to **HIGH** pressure for 8 minutes. Make sure the steam valve is in the "Sealing" position.

2 When the cooking time is up, quick-release the pressure. Set a colander in the sink and pour the potatoes and kale into the colander. Let the vegetables sit and cool for a few minutes; letting the steam evaporate will make the potatoes fluffier when you mash them.

3 While the vegetables cool, return the pot to the appliance, add the butter, select **SAUTÉ,** and adjust to **NORMAL/MEDIUM** heat. When the butter has melted, add the green onions and cook until tender, 1 minute. Add the milk or cream and bring to a simmer, 1 minute. Press **CANCEL**.

4 Return the potatoes and kale to the pot and mash with a potato masher until the potatoes are mostly smooth. Season with salt and pepper.

BROCCOLI WITH LEMON GARLIC DRESSING

· · · · · · · · · ·

Serves 4

ACTIVE TIME	FUNCTION	TOTAL TIME	RELEASE
5 minutes	Pressure	15 minutes	Quick

The Instant Pot makes perfect crisp-tender steamed broccoli in the time it takes for the appliance to come up to pressure, so you just set it to zero minutes and release the pressure as soon as it beeps. Cooking whole garlic in the steaming liquid mellows its sharpness and makes a great base for the creamy lemon dressing.

4 medium garlic cloves, unpeeled, left whole

1 pound broccoli, cut into 1- to 1½-inch florets, stems thinly sliced

2 tablespoons fresh lemon juice

1 teaspoon Dijon mustard

¼ cup olive oil

Salt and freshly ground black pepper

1 Place 1 cup warm water and the garlic in the pot. Set a steamer basket in the pot and place the broccoli in it. Lock on the lid, select the **PRESSURE COOK** function, and adjust to **HIGH** pressure for 0 minutes. Make sure the steam valve is in the "Sealing" position.

2 When the cooking time is up, quick-release the pressure. Transfer the broccoli to a large serving bowl. Remove the steaming basket from the pot. Transfer the garlic to a cutting board, discard the peels, and chop the cloves. In a medium bowl, combine the garlic, lemon juice, and mustard. Gradually whisk in the oil.

3 Toss the broccoli with the dressing and season with salt and pepper.

Tasty Tip: Substitute cauliflower or sliced carrots for half the broccoli, if desired. The cooking time will be the same.

STEAMED ARTICHOKES WITH LEMON-DIJON DIPPING SAUCE

· · · · · · · · · ·

Serves 4

ACTIVE TIME	FUNCTION	TOTAL TIME	RELEASE
5 minutes	Pressure, Sauté	30 minutes	Quick

The Instant Pot is every artichoke lover's dream—you can steam the tough vegetable in just 10 minutes and make a buttery garlic-Dijon dipping sauce all in the pot! You can fit 4 smallish (10-ounce) artichokes or 3 medium (12-ounce) artichokes in the pot; either way, it will serve four.

4 (10-ounce) whole artichokes, rinsed and drained

½ cup (1 stick) unsalted butter, at room temperature

2 garlic cloves, chopped

2½ tablespoons fresh lemon juice

1 tablespoon Dijon mustard

Salt and freshly ground black pepper

1 Trim the artichoke stems to within 1 inch of the base. Place a trivet or steamer basket in the pot and add 1½ cups warm water. Place the artichokes stem-side down on the trivet. Select the **PRESSURE COOK** function and adjust to **HIGH** pressure for 10 minutes. Make sure the steam valve is in the "Sealing" position.

2 When the cooking time is up, quick-release the pressure. To test for doneness, pull a leaf from near the center of an artichoke and scrape the tender bottom of the leaf off with your teeth; the flesh should come away easily. If they're not done, lock on the lid and cook under **HIGH** pressure for a minute or so more.

3 Transfer the artichokes to serving plates with tongs, cover loosely, and set them aside. Remove the trivet from the pot and discard the cooking water. Return the pot to the appliance. Select **SAUTÉ** and adjust to **MORE/HIGH** heat. Add the butter and garlic to the pot and cook until the garlic is sizzling and fragrant, 1 minute. Press **CANCEL**. Whisk in the lemon juice and mustard. Season with salt and pepper. Pour the butter mixture into dipping bowls and serve with the artichokes.

Tasty Tip:
Add slices of lemon and garlic to the steaming water to subtly infuse the artichokes with more flavor.

INDIAN-STYLE SPAGHETTI SQUASH

. . . .
Serves 4

ACTIVE TIME	FUNCTION	TOTAL TIME	RELEASE
10 minutes	Pressure, Sauté	40 minutes	Quick

Baking spaghetti squash takes at least an hour, but steaming it takes just 8 minutes under pressure in the Instant Pot. In this two-step recipe, squash halves are first steamed and then a spice butter is made in the pot using the **SAUTÉ** function to finish the squash. It makes a wonderful low-carb side dish for grilled meat or curries.

1   medium (2½-pound) spaghetti squash, halved lengthwise and seeded

3   tablespoons unsalted butter or ghee

1½ teaspoons brown mustard seeds

1   teaspoon cumin seeds

3   medium garlic cloves, chopped

1   medium tomato, chopped

Salt and freshly ground black pepper

Tasty Tip:

For spaghetti squash to pair with Italian meals, substitute 1 tablespoon chopped fresh oregano for the mustard and cumin seeds and proceed with the recipe as directed.

1 Place a trivet in the bottom of the pot and add 1½ cups cold water. Place the squash halves cut-side up in the pot. Lock on the lid, select the **PRESSURE COOK** function, and adjust to **HIGH** pressure for 8 minutes. Make sure the steam valve is in the "Sealing" position.

2 When the cooking time is up, quick-release the pressure. Transfer the squash to a cutting board. Drag a fork crosswise over the squash to scrape out the flesh into strands; discard the skins. Place the squash in a large serving bowl and cover with foil.

3 Discard the steaming water, dry out the pot, and return it to the appliance. Put the butter or ghee in the pot, select **SAUTÉ**, and adjust to **NORMAL/MEDIUM** heat. When the butter has melted, add the mustard seeds and cumin seeds and cook, stirring frequently, until the seeds begin to pop, 1 minute. Add the garlic and tomato and cook until fragrant, 1 minute. Press **CANCEL**.

4 Pour the butter mixture over the squash. Season with salt and pepper and toss with tongs to combine. Serve immediately.

SMOKY COLLARD GREENS OR KALE

....
Serves 4

ACTIVE TIME	FUNCTION	TOTAL TIME	RELEASE
15 minutes	Sauté, Pressure	30 minutes	Natural + quick

This quick Southern side dish gets its smoky flavor from bacon and smoked Spanish paprika. You can make a vegetarian version by omitting the bacon (add 1 tablespoon canola oil to the onion) and using vegetable broth. Serve with the Carolina Pulled Pork on page 171, the Honey Barbecue Spareribs on page 189, or the Barbecue Tofu Sandwiches on page 97.

3 slices thick-cut pepper bacon, chopped

1 small yellow onion, chopped

3 medium garlic cloves, chopped

¾ cup store-bought chicken or vegetable broth, or homemade (page 227 or 226)

2 large (9-ounce) bunches collard greens or kale, tough center stems discarded, leaves torn

2 tablespoons cider vinegar or red wine vinegar

1 teaspoon smoked paprika

Salt and freshly ground black pepper

1 Select **SAUTÉ** and adjust to **NORMAL/MEDIUM** heat. Add the bacon and onion and cook, stirring occasionally, until the bacon is browned, 8 minutes. Add the garlic and sauté until fragrant, 45 seconds. Press **CANCEL**.

2 Add the broth and scrape up the browned bits on the bottom of the pot. Add the greens, vinegar, paprika, ½ teaspoon salt, and several grinds of pepper and toss with tongs to coat the greens with the liquid. Lock on the lid, select the **PRESSURE COOK** function, and adjust to **HIGH** pressure for 5 minutes. Make sure the steam valve is in the "Sealing" position.

3 When the cooking time is up, let the pressure come down naturally for 10 minutes and then quick-release the remaining pressure. Season with salt and pepper. Serve the greens immediately.

Tasty Tip: Make the recipe faster by using prechopped collard greens or kale; they're available where bagged lettuce and prepped veggies are found in the produce department. You will need a 10-ounce bag.

SWEET-AND-SOUR RED CABBAGE

· · · · · · · · · ·
Serves 6

ACTIVE TIME	FUNCTION	TOTAL TIME	RELEASE
10 minutes	Sauté, Pressure	30 minutes	Quick

This sweet-and-sour cabbage infused with caraway seeds is the perfect side dish for Fig-Glazed Ham with Dill Potatoes (page 185) or Herby Pork Chops with Butternut Squash (page 175). The recipe contains only 3 tablespoons of liquid; the rest of the moisture to bring the pot up to pressure is supplied by the cabbage as it breaks down—baking soda helps the process along.

1   **medium (2-pound) red cabbage**
2   tablespoons olive oil
½   **medium red onion, sliced**
1½ **teaspoons caraway seeds**
½   **teaspoon baking soda**
3   tablespoons red wine vinegar
1   **tablespoon brown sugar**
    Salt and freshly ground black pepper

1 Cut the cabbage into quarters. Cut out the hard, white core at the base of each quarter and discard. Shred the cabbage into ¼-inch-wide strips. Set aside.

2 Put the oil in the pot, select **SAUTÉ**, and adjust to **MORE/HIGH** heat. When the oil is hot, add the onion, caraway seeds, and baking soda and cook until tender, 4 minutes. Add the vinegar and brown sugar and press **CANCEL**.

3 Add the cabbage, ½ teaspoon salt, and several grinds of black pepper and toss to coat. (The pot will look very full, but the cabbage will wilt substantially as it cooks.) Lock on the lid, select the **PRESSURE COOK** function, and adjust to **HIGH** pressure for 5 minutes. Make sure the steam valve is in the "Sealing" position.

4 When the cooking time is up, quick-release the pressure. Season with salt and pepper, and serve.

Tasty Tip: For a richer dish, add 3 slices chopped bacon to the pot along with the onion in Step 2 and cook until crisp, 4 to 6 minutes. Drain off all but 1 tablespoon of the drippings before adding the cabbage.

SMOKY "BAKED" BEANS

. . . .

Serves 4 to 6

ACTIVE TIME	FUNCTION	TOTAL TIME	RELEASE
15 minutes	Pressure OR Slow, Sauté	50 minutes, plus soaking time	Natural

These beans have a delicious sweet-savory flavor without all the corn-syrupy sweetness of canned baked beans. Spanish chorizo adds a hit of heat, but it's optional.

2 cups dried great Northern beans, picked over and soaked overnight or quick-soaked (see page 225)

1 medium yellow onion, chopped

½ cup chopped dry-cured Spanish chorizo (2½ ounces; optional)

Salt and freshly ground black pepper

¼ cup ketchup

¼ cup lightly packed brown sugar

3 tablespoons molasses

2 tablespoons cider vinegar

1 Drain the beans and place them in the pot. Add 2¾ cups water (just enough to cover the beans), the onion, chorizo, 1 teaspoon salt, and several grinds of pepper. Lock on the lid, select the **PRESSURE COOK** function, and adjust to **HIGH** pressure for 6 minutes. Make sure the steam valve is in the "Sealing" position. (Or you can **SLOW COOK** it—see below.)

2 When the cooking time is up, let the pressure come down naturally for about 20 minutes. Ladle off 1 cup of the cooking liquid and discard.

3 In a small bowl, mix the remaining ingredients and add to the beans. Select **SAUTÉ** and adjust to **NORMAL/HIGH** heat. Simmer, stirring frequently, until the sauce has thickened, 5 minutes. Press **CANCEL**. Season with salt and pepper and serve.

Tasty Tip: To start with unsoaked beans, increase the water in Step 1 to 3½ cups. Increase cooking time to 35 minutes in Step 1. Proceed with the recipe as directed, removing most of the cooking liquid in step 2.

Slow Cook It: Start with 2 cups dried (unsoaked) beans and increase the water to 6 cups. In Step 1 select **SLOW COOK**, adjust to **NORMAL/MEDIUM** heat, and set for 10 to 11 hours. Lock on the lid set to "Venting," or use a pan lid that fits snugly on the pot (see Helpful Equipment, page 18). You will need to ladle off 1¾ cups of the cooking liquid in Step 2.

PANTRY

RICE AND GRAINS

The **RICE** function on the Instant Pot is great if you like the convenience of pressing one button and walking away. The **RICE** function cooks rice under low pressure, so it takes twice as long or longer than choosing **PRESSURE COOK** and **HIGH** pressure. I opt for the latter and have found the best times for different types of rice using the manually set **PRESSURE COOK** function (see chart below).

The grain-to-liquid ratios in the chart yield perfectly cooked, fluffy rice with separate grains. If you prefer rice that is a bit moister (and easier to pick up with chopsticks), increase the liquid by a few tablespoons. Keep in mind that the ratios below assume you have rinsed your rice first. Rinsing rice thoroughly with cold water and draining it in a fine-mesh strainer removes excess starch and moistens the rice, so don't skip this step.

Adding a little oil or butter to the pot helps keep the grains separate and will minimize foam when releasing the pressure, but it's optional. I always add at least a few pinches of salt to improve the flavor of the rice or grains, but you can leave it out if you are watching your sodium intake.

For best results, cook at least 1½ cups dry rice or grains in the Instant Pot; this amount serves about 4 people. If you'd like to cook a smaller amount of rice, I recommend you cook it using the "pot in pot" method (see page 129, Chicken with Black Bean Garlic Sauce and Broccoli). At the end of the cooking time, always let the pressure release naturally for 10 minutes.

GRAIN	CUPS GRAIN (DRY, RINSED)	CUPS WATER	COOKING TIME (HIGH)	RELEASE
Short-grain (sushi) rice	1½ cups	1½ cups	4 minutes	10 minutes natural
Long-grain rice	1½ cups	1½ cups	4 to 6 minutes	10 minutes natural
Jasmine rice	1½ cups	1½ cups	4 minutes	10 minutes natural
California basmati rice	1½ cups	1½ cups	4 to 6 minutes	10 minutes natural
Long-grain brown rice	1½ cups	1½ cups	22 minutes	10 minutes natural
Short-grain brown rice	1½ cups	1¾ cups	22 minutes	10 minutes natural
Brown jasmine rice	1½ cups	1¾ cups	22 minutes	10 minutes natural
Black rice	1½ cups	1¾ cups	22 minutes	10 minutes natural
Red rice	1½ cups	1¾ cups	22 minutes	10 minutes natural
Quinoa	1 cup	1½ cups	1 minute	10 minutes natural
Freekeh	1 cup	1⅔ cups	5 minutes	Quick-release
Farro	1 cup	2½ cups	20 minutes	10 minutes natural (drain after cooking)

HOME-COOKED BEANS

For the best results, I recommend soaking dried beans before pressure cooking them, with a few exceptions. Presoaked beans cook more evenly and will not burst like unsoaked beans cooked under pressure do. You can soak beans by putting them in a large bowl with water to cover by 2 inches for 8 to 12 hours, or you can boil them with plenty of water for 1 minute and then let the beans soak for 1 hour in the hot liquid. Adding a teaspoon of salt to the soaking liquid helps to season them all the way through and helps keep the skins intact, but it is optional.

Beans continue to dry and harden as they age, so you'll occasionally come across beans that need longer than the suggested cooking time in the chart below. Always buy beans from a market that has a lot of food turnover to ensure you get beans that haven't been sitting around for years.

You can cook up to 1 pound (about 3 cups) dry, soaked beans in the 6-quart Instant Pot, but the pot will be very full, and beans expand as they cook. For safety and for the most even cooking, I recommend cooking no more than 1½ to 2 cups dried beans in the Instant Pot at a time.

To cook soaked beans, drain and rinse them, and place them in the pot with enough water to cover the beans by at least ½ inch. Add 1½ teaspoons salt, a chopped onion, a few garlic cloves, a bay leaf, or epazote (see Tasty Tip, page 39), if desired. Lock on the lid, select the **PRESSURE COOK** function, and adjust to **HIGH** pressure, following the times below. When the cooking time is up, let the pressure release naturally for at least 10 minutes. This will minimize busted beans and will finish cooking the beans slowly, a crucial step for tender beans with creamy interiors and skins that hold their shape. Remove the lid and taste the beans. If you feel they are not done, select **SAUTÉ**, adjust to **NORMAL/MEDIUM** heat, and simmer, uncovered, until the beans are done to your liking.

Cooked beans store well in the refrigerator for up to 5 days and in the freezer for up to 3 months. For convenience, I store beans in 1½-cup portions (the average amount in a can of drained beans) in zip-top freezer bags and lay them flat in the freezer for the most efficient storage.

SOAKED BEANS	COOKING TIME
Black-eyed peas	4 minutes
Black	8 minutes
Pinto	6 to 7 minutes
Kidney	7 to 8 minutes
Cannellini	5 to 6 minutes
Chickpea	8 to 10 minutes
Great northern	6 minutes

HOMEMADE VEGETABLE BROTH

. . . .

Makes about 8 cups

ACTIVE TIME	FUNCTION	TOTAL TIME	RELEASE
5 minutes	Pressure OR Slow	1 hour 20 minutes (if using Pressure)	Natural

The basic mix of onion, carrots, and celery makes a clear broth with a neutral flavor that's ideal as a springboard for soups and sauces. Other vegetables can certainly be added—mushrooms, garlic, leeks, fennel, tomatoes, and red bell peppers all make lovely vegetable broth. Do avoid vegetables from the brassica family such as cabbage, cauliflower, and broccoli, as they'll lend a skunky note to the broth.

1 medium yellow onion, chopped

2 carrots, roughly chopped

2 celery ribs, roughly chopped

1 tablespoon tomato paste

2 sprigs fresh thyme

1 bay leaf

1 Place the onion, carrots, celery, tomato paste, thyme, and bay leaf in the pot. Add 8 cups cold water.

2 Lock on the lid, select the **PRESSURE COOK** function, and adjust to **MORE/HIGH** pressure for 20 minutes. Make sure the steam valve is in the "Sealing" position. When the cooking time is up, let the pressure come down naturally for about 30 minutes. (Or you can **SLOW COOK** it—see below.)

3 Strain the broth through a fine-mesh sieve and discard the vegetables. Refrigerate the broth until cooled completely. Store in an airtight container in the refrigerator for up to 5 days or in the freezer for up to 3 months.

Slow Cook It: In Step 2, select the **SLOW COOK** function and adjust to **NORMAL/MEDIUM** heat for 7 to 8 hours. Lock on the lid set to "Venting," or use a pan lid that fits snugly on the pot (see Helpful Equipment, page 18).

HOMEMADE CHICKEN BROTH

• • • • • • • • • • • • • • •

Makes 8½ cups

ACTIVE TIME	FUNCTION	TOTAL TIME	RELEASE
5 minutes	Pressure OR Slow	about 1½ hours (if using Pressure)	Natural

The Instant Pot extracts every last bit of flavor and collagen from the bones. Use raw bones and chicken parts that are on sale—drumsticks are often the cheapest and give wonderful body to the broth. Including the onion skin gives the broth a deep golden color. Be patient and let the pressure come down naturally; if you quick-release, you'll encounter greasy spattering that's difficult to clean up.

3 pounds chicken parts (wings, backs, drumsticks)

1 medium yellow onion, roughly chopped with skin, root discarded

2 large carrots, roughly chopped

2 celery ribs, roughly chopped

3 medium garlic cloves

1 bay leaf

1 Place the chicken, onion, carrots, celery, garlic, and bay leaf in the pot. Add 8 cups cold water. Do not fill the pot over two-thirds full. Lock on the lid, select the **PRESSURE COOK** function, and adjust to **HIGH** pressure for 30 minutes. Make sure the steam valve is in the "Sealing" position. (Or you can **SLOW COOK** it—see below.)

2 When the cooking time is up, let the pressure come down naturally for about 30 minutes. Strain the broth through a fine-mesh strainer into a large bowl; discard the solids. Refrigerate, uncovered, until cooled completely. Spoon off the fat that rises to the top and discard. Transfer the broth to airtight containers and refrigerate for up to 5 days or freeze for up to 3 months.

Slow Cook It: In Step 1, select the **SLOW COOK** function and adjust to **NORMAL/MEDIUM** heat for 8 to 9 hours. Lock on the lid set to "Venting," or use a pan lid that fits snugly on the pot (see Helpful Equipment, page 18).

HOMEMADE BEEF BROTH

. . . .

Makes about 8 cups

ACTIVE TIME	FUNCTION	TOTAL TIME	RELEASE
15 minutes	Pressure OR Slow	2 hours (if using Pressure)	Natural

Use a mix of meaty beef bones such as oxtails, shanks, and marrow bones for the best flavor and texture. Broiling the bones adds a rich, roasted flavor, but it's an optional step.

3 **pounds meaty beef bones and marrow bones**

Salt and freshly ground black pepper

1 **medium yellow onion, coarsely chopped**

2 **large carrots, coarsely chopped**

2 **celery ribs, coarsely chopped**

1 **bay leaf**

1 Preheat the broiler and adjust the oven rack so that it is 6 inches below the broiling element. Line a rimmed baking sheet with foil and spray with cooking spray. Season the bones generously with salt and pepper and arrange them in a single layer on the prepared baking sheet. Broil until well browned, 6 to 8 minutes. Flip the bones with tongs and broil until browned on the second side, 5 minutes more.

2 Transfer the bones and any browned bits and accumulated juices from the baking sheet to the pot. Add the onion, carrots, celery, and bay leaf to the pot. Pour 8 cups cold water over the bones and vegetables (do not pass the MAX line on the inside of the pot).

3 Lock on the lid, select the **PRESSURE COOK** function, and adjust to **HIGH** pressure for 45 minutes. Make sure the steam valve is in the "Sealing" position. (Or you can **SLOW COOK** it—see opposite.)

4 When the cooking time is up, let the pressure come down naturally for about 30 minutes. Strain the broth through a fine-mesh sieve, season with salt and pepper, and refrigerate until completely chilled.

5 Discard the hard fat on top of the broth before using. The broth will look like jelly; this is a good thing. Store in airtight containers in the refrigerator for up to 4 days or in the freezer for up to 3 months.

Tasty Tip: If you're making broth for Asian-style recipes, substitute 1 whole star anise for the bay leaf and season with soy sauce or fish sauce instead of salt at the end of cooking.

Slow Cook It: In Step 3, select the **SLOW COOK** function and adjust to **NORMAL/MEDIUM** heat for 8 to 12 hours. Lock on the lid set to "Venting," or use a pan lid that fits snugly on the pot (see Helpful Equipment, page 18).

ACKNOWLEDGMENTS

If it takes a village to raise a child, it takes a small city to produce a cookbook. Though it often feels like I'm alone in the kitchen for hours on end, really there were many who were there with me—some literally, others in spirit.

Thank you to my book editor, Stephanie Fletcher, for her cheerful guidance and patience with my sometimes-faulty ability to count to 6. Thank you to my agent, Jenni Ferrari Adler, whose faith in my talent and work ethic makes me blush with pride. Thanks to Anna Di Meglio at Double Insight for her help—the devil is in the details.

A great round of applause goes to my recipe testers. Liz Tarpy, I write this in every one of my books, but seriously, I could not do this without you. Big bottle of bubbly for you! Thanks also to Paige Carlson, Joy Church, Bee Talmadge, John Mechalas, Maia Paul, Andy Manning, and Cathie Schutz. Your hard work, eagle eye, and honest feedback make me a better recipe writer and a better cook.

Thanks also to my squad of willing tasters—Joe and Leena Ezekiel, Mark and Stacey Flaherty, Meredith Haynes, Dean and Abbey Boudouris, Rosemarie Torrence, Kathleen Bauer, and Mary Lockhart. Your feedback cannot be measured in words. Thank you for returning all those containers!

A big thanks goes out to my dear friend Mini, who was a willing helper in the kitchen until the very last. We miss you, Moo. And finally, to my husband, Gregor Torrence, who weathered the storm yet again. I love you, dear, and not just because you eat the fails.

INDEX

Note: Page references in *italics* indicate photographs.

C

D

E

More books with more recipes for your Instant Pot!

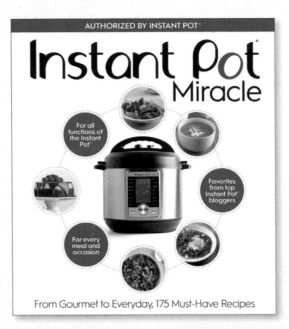

AUTHORIZED BY INSTANT POT®

Instant Pot® Miracle

For all functions of the Instant Pot®

Favorites from top Instant Pot® bloggers

For every meal and occasion

From Gourmet to Everyday, 175 Must-Have Recipes

AUTHORIZED BY INSTANT POT®

Instant Pot® ITALIAN

100 Irresistible Recipes Made Easier Than Ever

Ivy Manning

AUTHORIZED BY INSTANT POT®

Instant Pot® FAST & EASY

100 Simple and Delicious Recipes for Your Instant Pot

Urvashi Pitre

31901064534151

HMH hmhco.com